daiva

Also by K. Hari Kumar

India's Most Haunted: Tales of Terrifying Places
Dakhma: A Novel

daiva

Discovering *the* Extraordinary World *of* Spirit Worship

K. HARI KUMAR

**HARPER
NON-FICTION**

First published in India by Harper Non-fiction
An imprint of HarperCollins *Publishers* 2024
4th Floor, Tower A, Building No. 10, DLF Cyber City,
DLF Phase II, Gurugram, Haryana – 122002
www.harpercollins.co.in

2 4 6 8 10 9 7 5 3 1

Copyright © K. Hari Kumar 2024

P-ISBN: 978-93-5489-974-4
E-ISBN: 978-93-5489-970-6

The views and opinions expressed in this book
are the author's own and the facts are as reported by him,
and the publishers are not in any way liable for the same.

K. Hari Kumar asserts the moral right
to be identified as the author of this work.

All rights reserved. No part of this publication may be reproduced,
stored in a retrieval system, or transmitted, in any form or by any means,
electronic, mechanical, photocopying, recording or otherwise,
without the prior permission of the publishers.

Typeset in 10.5/13.5 Adobe Garamond Pro at
Manipal Technologies Limited, Manipal

Printed and bound at
Manipal Technologies Limited, Manipal

This book is produced from independently certified FSC® paper to ensure
responsible forest management.

To Tulu Appe (Mother Tulu)

Omens are a language, it's the alphabet we develop to speak to the world's soul, or the universe's, or God's, whatever name you want to give it.
—Paulo Coelho, *The Alchemist*

Contents

How the Journey Began   xi

PART 1
In Search of Satyolu

1.	The Land of Tuluvas	3
2.	Divination, Spirit Possession and Spirit Dance Forms	14
3.	Spirit Worship	24
4.	The Spirits	31
5.	The Origin of Bhutas	38
6.	The Sacred Realm	48
7.	The Ritualistic Dance	57
8.	Steps Involved in Kola	61
9.	Nudi Panpunna—The Justice of the Spirit Deities	86
10.	Seeking the Satyas	95

Part 2

The Stories of Satyolu

1.	Satyamma Kallurti and Beera Kalkuda	105
2.	Panjurli—The Boar Deity	123
3.	Koragajja	148
4.	Koti Chennaya—The Story of the Warrior Brothers	154
5.	Pilichandi	173
6.	Manthradevate	180
7.	The Story of Siri	185
8.	Jumadi	201
9.	The Fearsome Spirits	207
10.	Kordabbu and Thanimaaniga	213
11.	Bobbarya	218
12.	The Royal Deities	221
13.	Mother Goddess	231
	Acknowledgements	237
	Bibliography	241

How the Journey Began

March 2023
Pune

MANY MOONS AGO, AS I EMBARKED UPON A fulltime career in writing and filmmaking, my dear mother visited several astrologers in a bid to ascertain my planetary alignments. You see, I had read *The Alchemist*; she hadn't. To any sane mind, the decision to give up a well-paying, comfortable corporate job was perceived as clouded by passion. She was, of course, understandably concerned for her only son, who was about to plunge into the perilous depths of a literary career, in search of rare pearls amidst rusted shipwrecks and hungry sharks. While the words of most astrologers were as old and familiar as sea shanties, there were a few insights that piqued my interest.

I must make it clear that the advice offered was not magical in any sense, but rather, a collection of age-old wisdom and repetition, similar to the counsel dispensed by most elders when one is faced with life's challenges. Among their suggestions was a visit to our family deity, or kuladevata. Additionally, as a Tulu Nadu native, I was encouraged to discover our family's native serpent grove or the moolasthana of our naaga, and to find out if any daivas were once worshiped by my ancestors when they lived there, but may have been forgotten in the intervening years. Now this was an impossible task because my direct ancestors had left the native land over a century ago.

Intriguingly, an oracle even suggested that my profession as a writer would have some connection with the undead, owing to the karmic legacy of my forefathers, and the influence of a feminine spirit deity or a mother goddess. These insights stirred something within me, igniting a desire to trace my bloodline and uncover the deities worshiped by my ancestors. However, my first couple of attempts to embark on this quest lacked a certain amount of determination required for such an undertaking. All I could find out after talking to the eldest members of my family (near and far) was that my ancestors may have come from somewhere around Kateel, Surathkal or Kunjoor in Karnataka. However, like Santiago in *The Alchemist*, the time hadn't come for the quest ... yet.

In 2019, while we were filming the web series '*Bhram*' in the secluded precincts of Chail, Himachal Pradesh, the topic of the daivas and their divine justice made a comeback into my life. One of the main actors opined that the functions of the fictitious village deity that we had created for the story resembled that of the daivas of Tulu Nadu. At that time, he didn't know that my ancestors came from the region. It was a serendipitous revelation that resonated within the corridors of my consciousness, planting the seeds for the future quest that I would take up in 2023.

Three years down the line, in 2022, an opportunity unfolded that would unexpectedly pave the way for a unique exploration of my roots. This came in the form of an invitation to feature

How the Journey Began

on the *The Ranveer Show* podcast, hosted by the popular Indian content creator, Ranveer Allahbadia. However, this occurred at a time when I had completely retreated into a cocoon. Earlier that year, we had lost a baby and my paternal grandmother (whose stories had inspired me to become a writer). The incidents broke our hearts. Physically, I wasn't well either because of constant lower back pain that was keeping me homebound. Most of the time I was withdrawn from the world. I wasn't myself anymore. However, something urged me to emerge from the shell and record the podcast.

As fate would have it, this podcast marked a turning point in my narrative. During our conversation on Indian horror and the role of spirits in Indian folklore, Ranveer delved into the backstory of my formative years, probing the nuances of its influence on my journey as a genre writer. A chance remark about North Kerala's famous theyyam slipped from my lips, opening a gateway to a broader discussion. In an attempt to provide a visual reference to the diverse audience of his podcast, I drew parallels between theyyam and the cinematic portrayal of kola in *Kantara*, a widely recognized film from the year. This impromptu connection stirred Ranveer's interest, steering our dialogue toward a totally unplanned direction—to the cultural realms of Kola and the time-hounoured tradition of spirit worship of Tulu Nadu.

After the podcast recording in Versova, I jogged into a vegetarian restaurant in Andheri. That day, finding my usual spot overcrowded, I opted for another restaurant where I could indulge in my customary idli immersed in flavourful sambhar. To my surprise, a familiar visage greeted me behind the cashier. It was a framed photograph of Kateel's Durgaparameshwari. This was no ordinary picture of any goddess; she was the presiding deity of the very place I had just discussed on the podcast, the place where my ancestors likely resided over 150 years ago. This unforeseen encounter acted as a compelling omen, beckoning me towards Tulu Nadu and instigating the commencement of a personal quest to unearth the satya or the truth, hidden within the forgotten pages of my ancestral heritage.

A voice called to me, but I didn't know what it was—my rational mind would want to call it a thirst for truth and knowledge but the writer in me tells me romantically it was fate. For indeed, all my stories revolve around the theme of destiny and how unseen spiritual elements lead you to fulfil a prophecy. What followed was an adventure, a quest for knowledge and fulfilment that led me to explore numerous kolas, sthaanas, naagamandalas, temples and villages along the western coast, where my forefathers may have once lived.

As I delved deeper into the traditions of Tulu Nadu, I became increasingly fascinated by the worship of daivas. The very mention of a daiva would send goosebumps to those who believe in the spirit deities. Such is the power of devotion. Daiva aaradhane or the worship of spirit deities is integral to Tulu culture. My quest to find out about my roots drove me, and ultimately inspired me to pen this book, a tribute to the rich cultural heritage of Tulu Nadu.

My purpose in writing this book is not to present an academic treatise on daiva aaradhane, nor is it a critical analysis of the subject or a commentary on the present day politics surrounding it. I am neither a practicing expert nor a scholarly erudite to impart such knowledge to you. Instead, I seek to embark on a personal journey, as a migrant Tuluva, a writer of genre inspired from folklore, to unravel the mysteries of the spirit world and trace my roots in the land of the naagas and daivas. I have barely touched upon the common ritualistic aspects of this worship, but more importantly, I have tried to probe into the spiritual aspects of folk beliefs. This book should serve as a humble introduction to the daivas for specially those who

How the Journey Began

are not familiar with them, including migrant Tuluvas whose children may not know much about their rich cultural heritage. For those interested in delving deeper, I will also include a list of recommended further reading at the end of the book. As for my regular readers who are familiar with my past works, which have explored the realms of horror and speculative fiction, you may be wondering why I, as a writer of such dark fiction, have chosen to delve into the world of folklore and mythology of Tulu Nadu. Allow me to offer three reasons.

Firstly, as an Indian writer in English and Hindi, I draw inspiration from the rich and fascinating folklore of our country. While stories from our Puranas are recognized worldwide, much of the folk and dalit mythology has yet to reach a broader audience. The tales of the daivas, naaga, siri, and baidyarlu, deeply woven into the fabric of Tulu Nadu, have always captivated my imagination.

Secondly, the concept of a sacred realm inhabited by spirit deities is not just limited to Tulu Nadu, but it is a universal concept, transcending cultural boundaries and resonating with readers and viewers alike. Yes, the medium, the legend, and the ritualistic elements may be different, but the core belief remains universal. As a writer whose entire body of work revolves around entities that reach out from beyond the veil, I find myself compelled to explore this subject matter.

Lastly, the allure of the daivas themselves is simply too strong to resist. Their enigmatic and often spellbinding presence is a source of both fascination and devotion, and I am eager to share my personal experiences and insights with you, dear reader.

In the pages that follow, I request you to perceive my intentions with utmost clarity. It is not my desire to impose upon you the shackles of traditional folk beliefs or convictions; instead, I extend to you a heartfelt invitation into a sacred realm where the extraordinary intricately interlaces itself with the fabric of the ordinary.

Let these pages serve as a resplendent beckoning, an ethereal embrace of the enigmatic, to traverse uncharted waters, and to unearth the dormant profundities nestled within the recesses of our very own motherland. Even for those who may not subscribe to beliefs in ethereal elements like the spirits, they can certainly appreciate the mesmerizing folktales of Tulu Nadu and artistry of kola.

It is my sincerest aspiration that as you traverse the shared dimension of my learnings, we might forge a profound communion—a bridge that gracefully spans the chasm between the seen and the unseen, the known and the unknown, the worldly and the spiritual. Together, let us begin an expedition, wherein the enchantment of Tulu Nadu's daivas melds harmoniously with the intricate mosaic of its people's lives. In this symbiotic interplay, let the mystical dance of the daivas intertwine with the vibrant hues of our mortal existence, illuminating our paths with revelations about Tulu Nadu's spirit deities or as they say in Tulu—Satyolu.

PART I
In Search of Satyolu

1
The Land of Tuluvas

BEFORE WE BEGIN TALKING ABOUT DAIVAS, IT IS important to introduce the reader to the Tulu language, the geography and history of the land of Tulu-speaking people. The rolling hills and lush green coast of Tulu Nadu (also spelled as Tulunaad), located in the southwestern part of India (coastal Karnataka and northern Kerala), comprise a unique region that is a conflux of culture and history. Throughout the annals of time, Tulu Nadu has resided between the meandering waters of the Gangavalli River in the north and the cascading currents of the Chandragiri River of Kasaragod in the south. These hallowed grounds are the very same that we now recognize as Dakshina Kannada, Udupi (Karnataka), and Kasaragod (Kerala). Home to the Tulu-speaking people, this land boasts of a rich and complex past that spans several centuries. Although the official state languages are Kannada (in Karnataka) and Malayalam (in Kasaragod), there are a few other languages spoken in this part of the country like Konkani, Koraga, Beary, etc. but Tulu is the most spoken language here.

In Indian mythology, the region of Tulu Nadu is said to be part of the Parashurama Kshetra, a land that is steeped in a rich blend of legends and lore. According to one legend, the mighty Lord Parashurama, who had vanquished the Kshatriya clans in twenty-one fierce battles, granted all his lands to the venerable sage Kashyapa. Seeking a new abode, the illustrious sixth incarnation of Vishnu embarked on a rigorous penance to invoke the blessings of Lord Shiva. In response, Shiva directed Parashurama to take up residence in the verdant land towards the south, for he himself was preparing to take on the incarnation of Manjunatha. As Parashurama gazed in that direction, his eyes were greeted by a vast expanse of sapphire-blue ocean, a sight that had never before met his gaze. The resolute Parashurama, undeterred by this unforeseen circumstance, called upon Varuna, the god of the sea, to part the waters. Parashurama hurled his formidable axe mightily across the sea, and the waters receded before him, revealing a new area of land that stretched from Gokarna to Kanyakumari. However, the land that emerged from the sea was salty and unsuitable for habitation. Parashurama invoked forth the mighty Naagaraja Vasuki, who spat forth holy poison that transformed the salty sterile land into a lush, verdant paradise. In a grand tribute to Vasuki's bravery and loyalty, all snakes were appointed as protectors and guardians of the land, a fitting homage to the land's divine origins.

This story varies as we go further south on the Indian map. While mythology may weave fantastical stories, evidence of human habitation has been unearthed in numerous archaeological sites, dating back to the Neolithic era. This land has been a melting pot of various cultural influences, including the Kadambas, the Alupas, the Chalukyas, the Rashtrakutas, and the Vijayanagar Empire. The mention of the port 'Olokhoira' by Greek historians alludes to the valley ruled by the 'Alupa' or 'Alvakheda,' a testimony to the antiquity of the region. This is the land that gave birth to Dvaita Philosophy that would inspire several other schools of thought in Hinduism. The Beary community, which was once engaged in maritime trade, stands as one of the earliest Muslim settlements in India, boasting a rich history that spans over 950 years.

In the sixteenth century, the Portuguese opened a trade route along the coast of Tulu Nadu, facilitating increased contact between the Tulu-speaking people and Europeans. This interaction had a profound effect on the region, with new ideas, technologies and cultural practices introduced, adding to the region's already diverse mosaic.

Despite the influence of the Portuguese and other outside forces, the Tulu-speaking people have maintained a strong sense of cultural identity over the centuries. This is evident in the Tulu language, which has a unique grammar and vocabulary that sets it apart from other South Indian languages. Tulu Nadu is also home to a rich tradition of folk art, music and dance, which reflects the region's history and cultural heritage. The 'Yakshagana', a traditional dance-drama form, is a particularly important cultural practice.

In the verdant region of Tulu Nadu, the cultivation of coconut and areca nut reigns supreme, producing an abundance of these products that are not only exported throughout India but also beyond its shores. As a result, the products of the mentioned crops are an integral part of worship of daivas and naagas. Of course, this also shapes the culinary traditions of Tulu Nadu. The cuisine is a mélange of flavours and spices, with locally sourced ingredients giving it a unique character. A plethora of vegetarian and non-vegetarian dishes can be found in Tulu Nadu, ranging from the cylindrical leaf-moulded moode (a type of idli) to kori rotti (a spicy chicken curry served with crispy rice wafers). Another popular dish is the soft rice pancakes called neer dosa. Neer means water and this dish derives its name from the watery consistency of its batter. Then there is the savory coconut-based curry called gashi, made with either fish or vegetables. Three of the most popular evening snacks from the region are ambode, buns and goli bajje. However, when in Mangaluru, to overlook the tempting allure of charmuri (a tangy treat made from puffed rice) and gadbad icecream would be a gastronomic omission akin to a culinary sin.

Tulu Nadu, apart from its cultural prominence, also holds a pivotal position in the economy of India. The bustling port city of Mangalore has been a vital center for commerce and trade for centuries, boasting a thriving industrial sector and a growing tourism industry. On the other hand, Udupi is of great importance in Indian heritage, housing the Ashtamathas of Madhvacharya and the revered Udupi Shri Krishna temple. The region of Karla (Karkala) is home to the St. Lawrence Shrine Basilica, the monumental Gomateswara statue, and the ancient Durga Parameshwari temple of Belmannu. Moodbidri is renowned for its Jain temples, particularly the Saabira Kambada Basadi, known as the temple of a thousand pillars. Many budding artists find inspiration from Mookambika in Kundapura (erstwhile South Canara), while Dharmasthala and Kukke Subramanya in the southern part of the region attract thousands of visitors. Masjid Zeenath Baksh, an ancient mosque crafted from wood, stands as one of the oldest mosques in the Indian subcontinent. As we journey further south and cross the border into Kerala, we encounter Kasaragod, known as the Sapta Bhasha Sangama Bhumi, meaning 'the land where seven languages converge'. Indeed, Tulu Nadu has long been a melting pot of diverse cultures throughout its history.

Despite the relentless force of urbanization that has propelled the migration of people to the cities or outside, and the looming peril of globalization and consumerism that has coerced many to assimilate Western lifestyles, the age-old customs and practices that render Tulu Nadu its unique character continue to persist. There are also concerted efforts to preserve and promote these customs which draw hordes of visitors from across Tulu Nadu and beyond, keeping alive the legacy of this region.

Tulu Language

A language, as Mae Rita aptly put, is the roadmap of culture, revealing the essence of its people's past and present. In the context of Tulu, this statement holds true, for despite the continuous influx of external forces over the centuries, the Tulu language has persevered, retaining its essence and integrity. The language sets this region apart from its neighbours. Tulu is one of the five major Dravidian languages, alongside Tamil, Telugu, Kannada and Malayalam, and has a rich literary and cultural heritage. It is spoken by over 1.8 million people (2011 census) primarily in the South Indian state of Karnataka and the northern part of Kerala. It is also spoken by a significant population in Mumbai and abroad, where many Tulu-speaking people have migrated for work. Thus, it can be argued that the actual number of Tulu speakers surpasses that of some official languages in the country. So, is it an official language recognized by the eighth schedule of our Constitution? Sadly, the answer is no. Tulu does not enjoy the status of an official language at present. However, there is a demand for Tulu's inclusion along with thirty-eight other regional languages.

The origin of the word 'Tulu' remains contested, with multiple accounts vying for legitimacy. Some early literature claims that the word is derived from tulabhara (a Hindu weighing ritual) performed by King Ramabhoja after accidentally killing a serpent, while *Keralolpati* proposes that the king Tulubhan Perumal was the inspiration. However, both accounts have been debunked for lack of evidence. The most widely accepted version is that the word Tulu signifies the language's soft, flowing, and watery nature. It could also be inspired from the wet tropical weather of the region surrounded by sea and water bodies. Nevertheless, the exact origins of the Tulu language remain shrouded in mystery, but it is believed to have emerged from Proto-Dravidian, the progenitor of all Dravidian languages, around 2000 BCE. As a six-year-old living in Delhi, I believed that the Tulu I spoke at home with my mother was the only variation of the language. It was only a matter of time before I started travelling and interacting with Tulu speaking people from different parts of the country. Besides Common Tulu, there exist dialects such as Shivalli Tulu, Jain Tulu, etc. The Common Tulu spoken in Mangalore differs significantly from that spoken by those in the northern and southern parts of the region, as well as migrants in Kerala, Bangalore or Mumbai.

As a child growing up in Gurgaon (Haryana), most of my classmates thought that I spoke Tamil because I came from the 'South'. I'd tell them that I understood Tamil but my mother tongue is Tulu. Sadly, when someone who owned an encyclopedia (we didn't have Wikipedia in the 90s) would tell me that Tulu was a dialect because it doesn't have an original script, that would really disappoint me. This is somewhat true. The Tulu language, while highly developed in its own right, curiously lacks an original script to call its own. However, the Tigaliri script that is in use today is actually a variation of the Grantha script, which was brought over by the Tulu Brahmins who had migrated to Kerala for the study of agama sastras. This script resembles letters from Malayalam and Sinhalese. As writing in Devanagari script on tali-ola (palm leaf) proved to be a difficult task, the scholars who had gone to study agama sastra, instead, adopted a variation of the Malayalam script to serve their purposes (Bhat, 1975, xii).

It is interesting to note, however, that despite the lack of a script, much of Tulu's rich folklore and cultural heritage has been successfully passed down through the generations via the oral traditions of its people. Tulu is renowned for its distinctive oral folklore and traditions. The paaddanas (paardanas), which we shall delve into in the next section, are an integral aspect of Tulu's oral literature and heritage. Paaddanas are also an integral component of the Tulu tradition of kola, the ritualistic dance performance in which dancers summon powerful spirit deities that have safeguarded the Tuluvas' land for centuries. Kola is thought to have originated as a way of appeasing and honouring these spirit deities. In my journey from the north to the southern part of Tulu Nadu, I have witnessed the awe with which kola is practiced in Tulu-speaking communities.

The veneration of spirit deities in Tulu Nadu, shielded by the natural barriers of the Western Ghats and the Arabian Sea, is a practice believed to have predated the aryanisation of the land. It is widely held that the region's unique geography has safeguarded its indigenous spirit worship and language from external influences. The exact origins of this tradition remain a mystery, and scholars have proposed various theories over the years. One such theory mentions of a king called Bhutala Pandyan who is also credited for introducing the 'aliyasantana' or matriarchal system in the region. This assumption would mean that bhuta worship is at least 1500 years old. While some experts maintain that the origin dates back to the fifteenth century, others argue that it is much older and may even have been present in the era before the invention of clothing by humans (Upadhyaya, 2002, p.no. 6-7).

One aspect of this time-honoured practice that has endured is the attire of the divine dancers who participate in these rituals. Though it has evolved over the centuries, their dress remains firmly rooted in the ancient customs of the region. The differences in the costume can be noted from the closing scene (top shot) in *Kantara* where the Panjurli daivas from two different eras meet at the sacred spot in the jungle.

Tulu Oral Tradition

Paaddanas (PäDdanas/Paardanas) are products of a pre-literate society; therefore, they are a cherished component of the region's oral tradition. They have been dutifully safeguarded and handed down orally through generations by some communities of Tulu people. In the written world, it was the efforts of Rev A. Manner, a Basel missionary, that initiated these narratives into the wider sphere, which ensured that their invaluable contents shall endure forevermore.

In Tulu culture, paaddanas is a manifestation of the folk song genre. Some of these narratives unravel the genesis of the spirits and chronicle their journey, and final ascension into the sacred realm of the spirits. The etymology of the term paaddanas is rooted in various theories, including its possible derivation from the Kannada word haadu (paadu in Tamil and Malayalam, the d is pronounced as in 'den') which means 'to sing' or even from the Sanskrit word padya, which signifies a part of a verse. Some scholars have derived the word from the Sanskrit term praarthana, which is a prayer or chant, however, it is dismissed by others as most narrative poems are not associated with rituals or prayers but rather with depiction of the deities' journeys.

The paaddanas were carefully transmitted through generations in the oral tradition by the Pambada, Nalike and Parava communities that perform the accompanying dance. While their precise origins remain elusive, the cultural significance of paaddanas is indisputable. Other paaddanas may also be rendered in the fields while tending to the paddy crop or tapping of toddy.

These chants serve to alleviate tedium and weariness, serving as a balm to soothe the strain of arduous labour.

In the second part of this book, I have explored several popular folktales rooted in paaddanas. Some of these tales, such as those of Kalkuda-Kallurti, Koti-Chennaya, Kordabbu-Thannimaaniga and Koragajja, revolve around the suppression of marginalized communities and their subsequent rebellion against their oppressors. Serving as a poignant reflection of the society from which they originated, these narratives vividly depict both its aspirations and its injustices.

The Tulu paaddanas, known for their varied lengths ranging from brief moments to lengthy hours, are delivered by the artist in parts, with an occasional interval. This is known as 'sandi'. While the terms paaddanas and sandi may be used interchangeably by some, sandi finds its roots in the term 'sandhi', meaning to join pieces together or a transition point. While paaddanas may represent the entire tale, sandis serve as different episodes or chapters within the complete story.

While Rev Manner has been acknowledged in the beginning of this chapter, it is the nameless individuals whose identities have dissolved into the vastness of the maya or sacred realm who merit the highest commendation for their invaluable contributions in passing on these lyrical accounts to posterity. To aid in the recollection of these lengthy compositions, the performer and their supporting vocalists utilize rhyme, alliteration and repetition. As mentioned previously, a supporting singer, usually a female, accompanies the artist during the performance of the paaddanas, with the alternating singing providing a welcome respite to both. Not all paaddanas may have sandis, however. The language employed by the artists of this folk tradition is imbued with an archaic charm, characterized by a sweetness that delights the senses, like drops of honey. Although the diction may appear straightforward at first glance, a keen ear will detect intriguing idioms and expressions interwoven throughout. The tones of the singers rise and fall in a distinct pattern, creating a hypnotic rhythm that lingers in the ears of the listener long after the ballad has ended. The repetitive sounds are believed to induce a hypnotic effect, fostering a focused and relaxed mental state. This altered state, marked by heightened suggestibility, and increased attention, facilitates the dancer's ability to what may be considered a trance.

Apart from paaddanas, kabite, uraal and bira are also part of the Tulu folk song tradition. These ballads and epic poems, passed down from generation to generation, offer a glimpse into a rich cultural heritage that endures despite the many challenges that its people have faced over the years.

Challenges

The tradition of paaddanas is declining as fewer people are singing the songs. This decline is due to fragmentation of agricultural lands and increased commercial use, as well as mechanization in the field. The documentation of the songs and conversations with the singers is crucial, and there is a need to preserve these oral traditions through print and digital platforms (Deccan Herald, 06 December 2022).

It is not just the folk music form but also the language that has faced significant challenges in the recent times, despite its impressive literary and cultural history. The language has been marginalized in education and media, and numerous Tulu speakers have switched to speaking Kannada (in Karnataka), Malayalam (in Kerala) or other languages in their daily lives. However, in recent years, there has been a renewed interest in Tulu language and culture, with efforts to promote its usage in schools and media. To be deemed a truly elevated mode of communication, a language must possess its own script. In the absence of an original script, a language's identity and prominence are likely to be undermined, making it susceptible to being overlooked as a mere dialect or even erased altogether. The absence of a script for a language not only hampers its development, but it also denies its speakers a rightful place in the realm of intellectual and cultural pursuits. Thus, the pursuit and propagation of the script for Tulu is crucial for preserving its essence and ensuring its continued growth and survival in the current age.

One of the organizations that have been actively working to promote Tulu language and culture is the Tulu Sahitya Academy, which was founded by the Karnataka government in 1994. The Academy has been tirelessly documenting and preserving Tulu literature and folklore, ensuring that the language's unique literary and cultural traditions are not lost.

The Tulu language boasts a rich history and cultural heritage that stretches back centuries. Despite the challenges it faces in modern times, various efforts are underway to safeguard and promote the language and its unique cultural and literary traditions. As Tulu evolves and adapts to the changing times, it remains a crucial part of south Indian culture and identity.

2

Divination, Spirit Possession and Spirit Dance Forms

DIVINATION AND SPIRIT POSSESSION ARE TWO supernatural concepts that have been deeply intertwined in many cultures and have existed ever since humankind decided to find a reason for their existence. These two supernatural phenomena have been part of many horror stories and films. The fact that these concepts are found all over the world speaks volumes about how the human mind is connected at a deeper subconscious level or at a primordial evolutionary level.

Divination

Divination has roots in the Latin word 'divinationem' that itself is derived from 'divinare' which means 'to be inspired by a divine deity or god'. Divination refers to the practice of seeking knowledge or guidance from divine sources. This could be through interpretation of omens, signs, or other forms of divinatory techniques. There are cases where those involved in the profession of astrology go into a trance and provide insight into a problem. It's essential to note that there is no scientific validity for such predictions or prophecies, and some practitioners of astrology themselves don't believe in them.

Spirit Possession

Spirit possession, on the other hand, involves a person becoming a vessel for a spirit or deity, allowing it to speak or act through the possessed person. When I speak of possession, the first thing that comes to an Indian's mind is Manjulika from *Bhool Bhulaiyya* (or in my case it is Naagavalli from *Manichitratazhu*). Well, that is also possession but it is of involuntary nature. What we see in most films and series are about people getting possessed by a spirit that is seeking revenge from a wrong-doer. Often termed as demonic possession in Hollywood films, some self-appointed paranormal experts are importing it into the Indian fold of things as well. In fact, I vaguely remember once hearing someone confidently claiming that possession 'always' happens in four stages. However, this book as well as our culture have nothing to do with the four stages of demonic possession described by Father Gabriele Amorth in his book *An Exorcist Tells His Story*. So, I want to make it very clear that when I say 'spirit possession' during the course of this book, I am strictly referring to those who become voluntarily possessed by spirits of deities, and this is not a demonic or negative phenomenon at all. The velichappad oracles of Kerala are an example, and so is the 'darshana' received by kola dancers of Tulu Nadu about whom we will talk in detail in this book.

The Common Ground

While divination and spirit possession practices may seem very different at first glance, they are often closely related in the way they are understood and practiced. In many cultures, divination is seen as a means of communicating with spirits or deities, and spirit possession is a key part of the divinatory rituals.

One way that divination and spirit possession intersect is in the idea that both practices involve a kind of trance or altered state of consciousness. In divination, the practitioner enters a trance-like state through meditation with or without the help of ritualistic herbs in order to interpret the signs or messages they receive from spirits. Similarly, in spirit possession, the person hosting the deity may enter a trance state in order to allow the deity to communicate or act through them.

Another way in which divination and spirit possession are related is in the idea of intermediaries between the human and supernatural (spirit) realms. In many cultures, diviners and spirit mediums are seen as intermediaries who can communicate with spirits or deities on behalf of the community. They may use divinatory techniques to interpret signs or messages from the supernatural realm, or they may become possessed by spirits or deities in order to receive guidance or solutions at the time of a great distress.

Spirit Dance Forms

The belief that spirits or ancestors possess the power to shape the lives of the living, and can intercede on their behalf with the divine, forms the foundation of spirit worship. The worshipper seeks to appease these spirits through elaborate rituals and ceremonies, hoping to garner their blessings. These spirits are believed to reside in natural objects such as trees, rocks and rivers, as well as in ancestral tombs and shrines. The indigenous cultures across the world consider dance to be a crucial component of spirit worship practices. Dance is also believed to possess the ability to connect people with the divine. Among these dances, spirit possession dances involve the dancer being taken over by a spirit or deity.

The Kalanga tribal dance, Amabhiza, originates in Zimbabwe's Matabeleland South Province. During the dance, which is performed during rain-asking ceremonies to appease the spirits of the rainmakers for a bountiful harvest, the dancers mimic horses' steps. The dance is accompanied by three drums, clapping and a whistle.

Kagura, a type of Shinto ritual ceremonial dance, derives its name from the contraction of the phrase 'kami no kura,' which means 'seat of god,' signifying the presence of gods (kami) during the practice. One of the main functions of kagura is chinkon, which involves a procession-trance process aimed at purifying and shaking the spirit. A female shaman typically performs the dance, obtaining an oracle from the god. During the performance, the dancer is believed to transform into a deity.

Yanvalou is a dance form associated with Haitian Vodou that originated in Benin, West Africa. It is performed in groups as a prayer, invoking deities and causing the dancers to lose consciousness and enter a state of trance. The dancers are believed to be possessed by loa, or spirits, and may perform movements and gestures that correspond to the particular loa with which they are possessed. The Nyau dance of Malawi is a traditional and deeply significant ritualistic dance performed by the Chewa people, particularly during cultural ceremonies and rites of passage. The masked performers are believed to channel the spirits of ancestors, acting as intermediaries between the physical and spiritual realms. In the Saghyang dance that originates in Bali, a spiritual force called *hyang* enters the body of the dancer. Some forms of Saghyang bear very close procedural resemblance to the kola. In all these dances, the costume bears a lot of importance. In the shamanic possession dances among the Tuvan people of Siberia, the shaman dons a costume made of eagle feathers, performing movements and gestures. The Barong dance, which also has some portions where the dancers enter a trance, have some of the most eye-catching costumes.

The Cham dance, also known as the God dance, is a remarkable and intimate performance unique to Tibetan Buddhism. Buddhist monks are the only ones permitted to perform it. Unlike ordinary dances, the Cham holds a significant religious meaning, serving as a form of meditation for both dancers and audience alike. Through the Cham dance, the monks offer their devotion, impersonating deities and protectors to protect and bless the people. As they perform, they are accompanied by the resounding melodies of traditional instruments—handheld drums, cymbals, large drums, blow horns, trumpets, and long trumpets—with chants and mantras rhythmically recited to enhance the experience. A similar musical offering can be seen in the kola, as we shall discover in this book. The Cham dance is performed at religious festivals, attracting visitors from even remote nomadic regions. The dance performed on auspicious occasions commemorates the Buddha and Dharma, serving as a powerful prayer for world peace and protection of all living beings. Similarly, in the Tuluvas' spirit dance, a daiva is invoked to protect the village or family conducting the kola or nema. In the early days of Buddhism, when most of the common people couldn't read or write, and printing was a luxury, dance became an important way to spread Buddhist teachings and blessings. Through the Cham dance, religious stories were brought to life before the audience's eyes, weaving them into the fabric of the culture.

Western View

Divination and spirit possession, despite their rich history and cultural significance, have long been viewed with suspicion or even contempt in the West. If the contempt rises from a rational point of view, I believe it is fine. To my mind, this disparagement cannot always be attributed to reason alone, but rather, may be a product of a certain narrow-mindedness and a failure to accept alternate systems of belief, namely those grounded in folk religion.

The rise of rationalism and individualism in Europe led to a particular understanding of the self as a rational and autonomous entity, capable of controlling one's thoughts and actions. This idea was at odds with the phenomenon of spirit possession, which was often seen as a threat to the rational and autonomous self, and therefore to the values of modern Western society.

Frequently characterized as primitive by outside observers, these practices have been stigmatized due to the enduring influence of Western colonialism and the suppression of indigenous spiritual traditions. It is for this reason that accounts of folk customs and rituals written by colonial surveyors are sometimes critical and dismissive in their tone.

In his thought-provoking article, 'Cultural Bias in the New England Puritans' Perception of (Native) Indians', anthropologist William S. Simmons reveals the deeply ingrained prejudices held by the Puritan migrants who arrived in New England in the 1620s. These immigrants believed that the indigenous people who had long inhabited the land worshipped demons, and held their religious leaders in contempt as witches. To these outsiders, the native people themselves were perceived as being possessed by evil spirits. Regardless of the observer's perspective, whether it was sympathetic or hostile, informed or uninformed, these prejudiced views were expressed as established facts in their writings. The

Cham dance, that I mentioned a while ago, is a sight to behold for foreign visitors today, who are entranced by the elaborate costumes and intricate decorations. Interestingly, it is believed that early travellers to Tibet mistook it for a 'devil dance,' given the wrathful form of the Tibetan protectors depicted in the dance. This again is similar to what the colonial writers called the ritual dance of the Tuluvas. The 'kola kattunaakkul' hailing from the Pambada, Parava, and Nalike communities, who are responsible for the preservation of this tradition, were also labeled as 'devil dancers' by the white man, when in reality they were the 'divine dancers' for the believers. The title of the earliest English work on the subject by A.C. Burnell, *The Devil Worship of the Tuluvas*, exemplifies this mindset. You see, just by translating the word 'Bhuta', you don't arrive at the conclusion that it is devil or any such evil entity (I will clarify this in the next chapter). Such observers were utterly disconnected from the folk culture, viewing it through a foreign lens that was dominated by a singular universal divine figure. They failed to grasp the profound sense of connection to the local deities, and the comfort they provided to believers in times of uncertainty or distress, simply because they lacked understanding of the culture. The way individuals perceive and interpret possession experiences is shaped by cultural expectations and beliefs. For example, in cultures where possession is viewed positively, individuals may be more likely to have positive emotional experiences during possession, while in cultures where it is viewed negatively, individuals may experience negative emotions such as fear or shame.

In the wake of Westernization and the advancement of scientific reasoning, the traditional customs and spiritual practices of non-Western societies have often been devalued and marginalized. Divination, spirit possession and ritual dances, in particular, have been frequently derided as irrational and primitive, relegated to the fringes of society and portrayed in sensationalized ways in the media. Those who have been raised in urbanized environments, whether in India or abroad, far removed from the traditions and beliefs of their ancestors, may look upon these practices with fear or suspicion, unable to comprehend the cultural and spiritual significance that they hold for others. Yet, it is essential to recognize that these practices may appear as mere superstitions or pseudoscience, but deeply rooted in the beliefs, values and worldviews of the people who practice them, especially from the marginalized communities who were left without access to 'higher ranking gods'. These practices offer a sense of connection to a spiritual realm (sometimes unknowingly) and a means of understanding the complexities of the world that is often lost in modern society's rationalist worldview. As a writer of genre and such speculative fiction, I can vouch for one thing—there's a lot more to this existence than what meets the eye. Just because we can't sense it doesn't mean we should dismiss it. The whole idea of a ritualistic dance and possession of a spirit may seem absurd to an outsider. However, through an understanding of these practices, one can begin to appreciate the rich cultural heritage of our land, and the diverse ways in which people make sense of the world around them.

Psychic Phenomenon in the West

The West may have been quite dismissive about the supernatural and paranormal, but it has also churned some of the finest piece of literature and cinema pertaining to that genre. Permit me to draw your attention to Spiritism, Spiritualism and Mediumship, three concepts that originate from the West and pertain to the afterlife and spirit possession. It is noteworthy that many of the paranormal phenomena and Hollywood movies that the West has produced find their roots in Spiritualism and Spiritism. The supernatural and paranormal have always fascinated the Western world; the believers in psychic phenomenon advance the notion of human souls transcending physical demise and engaging in communication with the living sphere through mediums or psychics (Remember the opening scene of *The Conjuring 2* where Lorraine Warren's character holds a séance to witness the Amityville murders?). This movement has attracted a fervent following, both within and beyond Western frontiers, and its adherents predominantly possess an ardent passion for social justice. During the late nineteenth century, trance mediums emerged as the cynosure of attention.

Trance Mediumship

Trance mediumship, frequently categorized as a variant of mental mediumship, entails the medium remaining fully cognizant during a communication session in which a spirit employs the medium's mind as a conduit for conveying messages. The spirit or spirits that are believed to communicate through the medium's mind influences their thoughts to convey the intended message. In the process, the medium sublimates their ego to allow the message to manifest. Simultaneously, the medium retains awareness of the thoughts transmitted and may even inject their biases into the message. During a deep trance, the medium may lack lucid recollection of all the messages imparted whilst in an altered state, necessitating the presence of an assistant to transcribe or otherwise record the medium's words. This is an important point that we should note as it can be used to explain the awe-inspiring phenomenon called 'moojemukkaal galige' in the ritualistic dance of kola.

Concluding Words

In this book, I do not intend to challenge rational thinking, which promotes a scientific temperament and safeguards people from vulnerability and exploitation. Similarly, I do not aim to question Western beliefs, as I firmly believe that our society has also greatly benefited from them. Our culture has always been inclusive and welcoming, and we have assimilated new ideas and practices, making them an integral part of our way of life and eventually, our culture and identity as 'Indians'. This embracing nature of our culture has also kept age-old traditions alive, though not in their original form, but they are still alive! Now, whether to believe in traditional rituals or not is an individual's personal choice, and we must respect that and embrace the fact. In my experience, I have witnessed people undergo profound changes. Circumstances sometimes turn believers into non-believers and non-believers into staunch believers. Let it be. In the end, we truly do not know where we are heading. Not even the most commercial spiritual leader can give you the right answer without hiding behind the veil of faith. But what impresses me most about daiva aaradhane is the fact that people, whether working in air-conditioned cubicles in top tech companies or hustling in the humid lanes of faraway cities, every year, thousands of them flock to their native places in Tulu Nadu to witness traditional jaatre, aarat, kola, nema, etc. Such traditions have kept the otherwise divided society bound by the ethereal thread of faith.

3

Spirit Worship

LAST YEAR I VISITED THE CITY WHERE I SPENT MY childhood, Gurgaon, to attend a literary event hosted by my alma mater. As was customary, I made it a point to catch up with old friends whenever I visited the city. Thus, on a balmy winter afternoon, I found myself ensconced in a quaint café in the bustling Galleria market, my senses lulled by the heady aroma of Irish coffee (trust me, this was an exception. The only coffee I love and drink is the filter kaapi). It was then that my school friend, Deva, while waiting for his cup of cappuccino, after talking about a lot of nostalgic things, brought up the topic of *Kantara*. Gushing over the film's brilliance, he extolled the virtues of the South Indian film industry over Bollywood. I lamented the monolithic label of 'South Indian' that did little justice to the rich diversity that pervaded the four distinct film industries of the South (It is actually six, if you include the lesser known Tulu industry of South Canara and Dollywood or the Deccani film industry of

Hyderabad). Thus began a conversation that would soon transport us to the mystical realm of kola and daiva aaradhane, and it was then that my friend posed a question that was both surprising and heartwarming, *'You are a Tuluva, right?'*

I nodded.

'Do people from your region really worship *ghosts*?' he asked.

I took a deep breath and let out a sigh. This was a question that many people have asked, including on some interviews and podcasts.

In the lexicon of the Tuluva people, 'bhuta' is not a word that is casually tossed around as a synonym for ghosts or evil spirits. In fact, the Tuluva people would argue that such an association with their traditional practices is deeply flawed and entirely misplaced. It is true that the word 'bhoot' (in most Indian languages) is commonly used to refer to ghosts or something that once existed but is now no more. Typical logic leads to the term 'dead' and anything dead can come back to haunt as a 'ghost'. Because people are scared of ghosts, they demarcate them as 'evil'. Due to this association, it's not difficult to see why bhuta-kola is often perceived by outsiders as the dance of the malevolent ghost, devil or demon.

However, such a definition falls far short of capturing the rich and complex cultural significance of 'bhuta' as it is understood by the Tuluva people. 'Bhuta' represents something altogether more profound, something that cannot be so easily dismissed or explained away as mere superstition or myth.

So, after a brief delay, I told my friend, 'Bhutas are not ghosts, dear. You can consider them as spirits of long-gone local legends and heroes that are worshipped to this day.'

'So, there is no supernatural force involved?' he asked out of curiosity.

I was pretty sure that he was recollecting the climax of that Kannada film which triggered this conversation. With a warm smile, I explained, 'Well, it is believed that there is a supernatural force but it is not evil or malevolent. Rather, it is considered divine in nature. This force enters the kola dancer.'

'Like in the film …'

Smile still in place, I said, 'Almost.'

In Sanskrit, the word Bhuta could mean 'the past', 'the spirit of the dead', 'the elements' or 'Shiva's attendants', while aaradhana denotes devotion or worship. So, bhuta-aaradhane may literally mean worship of these spirits.

It was at that moment that the attendant arrived with a steaming cappuccino for my companion and placed it on the desk. My friend reached for a sachet of sugar and, whilst adding it to the coffee, opined, 'Hari, I stumbled upon some stuff on the internet, alright? Some claimed that bhuta kola was a form of devil worship.'

'Indeed, I am afraid that is true.'

'So, these aren't ghosts, but rather devils?'

'No. I mean, it is true that some people had claimed it was devil worship, but actually, it is not like that.'

'I fail to understand. Why then did they call it the cult of devil worship?' he queried, his thick digits gripping the wooden stirrer.

'It is a result of religious misinterpretation and appropriation. What you read was likely influenced by the perspectives of colonial authors for whom the kola rituals seemed feral and satanic. It is possible that they based their initial impressions based on the views of their informants. They equated bhuta with Satan or, in broader terms, the devil.'

'Ah, that elucidates the matter. So, bhuta is not an impish spirit or the devil.'

'Correct, but they are feared by the worshippers too.'

'Why so?' he inquired, returning the stirrer to its tray.

'Because if provoked, sometimes these spirits may inflict harm.'

In that moment, the elbow of my cherished companion, by chance, made contact with the handle of the ceramic vessel that held the frothy cappuccino, causing it to plummet to the ground, breaking into countless fragments. A scant few droplets of the scalding brew, in a close shave, spattered onto the expanse of his beige polo shirt, barely skirting his bare brown arms. Subsequent to this incident, his words on the subject were muted. Possibly, he harboured fear.

Fear has forever been a tool employed by the aged to discipline the young. That is why most grandmothers regale kids with tales of ghosts and witches that would abduct disobedient kids who neglected to heed their parents or skipped bathing. I recollect that when I was six or seven-years-old, my *ajja* (grandfather) once caught me biting into a chakkuli (chakli or murukku, whatever you'd like to call it in your region). Basically, we call this way of eating 'made ampuna' in Tulu or 'jootha karke khaana' in Hindi. Ajja ensnared my left ear in his grasp and admonished me that children who bit into chakkuli or any snack would be abducted by a yakshi. He counselled me to rend them into fragments with the right hand and ingest them one at a time, like 'civilized' individuals. Even to this very day, I vow, I do not directly bite into any snack. Rather, I dismember them into smaller portions and deposit them, piece by piece, into my mouth. Of course, this tendency promotes hygiene especially while sharing food, but truth remains that the fear factor worked effectively in disciplining the child. Religion uses fear too.

The Basel Missionaries are credited with disseminating modern techniques of tile manufacturing, weaving, and for bringing the first printing press to the shores of coastal Karnataka in 1841, (Hindu, 2016). However, upon their arrival in coastal Karnataka two centuries ago, their dealings with the bhutas of Tulu Nadu were not harmonious, for they considered them to be devilish, the enemies of God, and proponents of evil. They appeared as pagan modes of worshiping nature or something far more sinister. According to their religious views, serving the bhutas was a sure way to eternal damnation. Their condescension and lack of appreciation of the bhutas' place in local culture is apparent as the people have been referred to as heathens in their annual reports (the forty-sixth report of the Basel German Evangelical missionary society in South-Western India for 1885, 1886). The colonial writers of the time also found the music of the kola rituals too loud and disharmonious, and the physicality of the performance too violent. They deemed it an offense to the sensibility and equated the idea of the numerous bhutas with that of the devil and demons. Come to think of it, it wasn't their fault. The missionaries may have feared burning in hell if they indulged in worshipping anyone except the one true God (mentioned in their scriptures), just like the natives feared the wrath of their many deities. The fear and belief are purely subjective. Thus, if you pick up any old book or articles about bhuta-aaradhane, you are likely to encounter the terms 'devil' or 'cult.' But now you know, just like my school friend, that bhutas are not evil ghosts or demons but spirit deities who are worshipped by the natives.

An excerpt from The Forty-Sixth Report of the Basel German Evangelical Missionary Society

Mr. Schaible describes an incident he met with during a demon festival in Reajala, S. E. of Karkal:

On the 2nd day whilst a procession of the Bhutas was arranged, the devil-dancer was arrayed in his tandry dress. The Catechist and myself began to preach. Then began the maddening tom-tom (musical intrusment), and torchlight in spite of broad daylight. Whilst this was going on the devil-dancer placed himself in front of us with the intention of acting as a spell on our sermon. Instead of getting alarmed we went on addressing him also, when he made himself scarce. The heat of the sun forced us to retire to the shadow of a tree, where the leading men of the place were listening to the oracle of the Bhutas through their devil-dancers. The president of the Yoga, who was the officiating priest, informed me, that it was customary to offer a nazir (a present) to important men, and asked whether I would accept of a cocoanut offered to the Bhuta. Remembering 1 Cor. 10, 20: 'But I say, that the things which the Gentiles sacrifice, they sacrifice to devils, and not to God, and I would not that ye should have fellowship with devils,' I declined the gift. Meanwhile the Bhutas, impatient at the interruption, called upon the president to listen to their say. The one shouted out a shower of blessings on rice, fruits and cattle, and finished by saying: 'In case of distress I am near at hand'.

The other Bhuta showed himself greatly displeased: 'My temple is on the point of collapsing,' he began, 'owls and bats have disputed with me my place of residence; they do not respect me, but live alongside of me. If my temple is not repaired, I shall leave the village, and endless plagues will remind you of your neglect.'

'I beg your forbearance', replies a temple trustee, 'consider what poor weak individuals we are, how often did we attempt to restore your temple, but were as often hindered.'

'Mind' replied the Bhuta, 'I am not going to be fed on excuses and broken promises; I wish for an answer as to whether you intend repairing my hovel or not. If you do, all right, I shall stay, otherwise my mind is settled on going.'

'Do not fall out with us, nor leave us, I most solemnly promise to execute your wish.'

4

The Spirits

A FEW YEARS BACK, I WAS INVITED TO JOIN A PANEL at a prestigious literature festival, and let me tell you, a horror panel getting a spot in a big literature festival felt like winning the lottery—or at least, like finding a ghost under your bed. Jokes apart, there I was, on the stage, watching my co-panelist eloquently speak about the usual Western supernatural creatures—blood-sucking vampires, broom-riding witches, and night-howling werewolves. I couldn't help but notice that when he began to delve into Indian entities, he was equating them with their Western counterparts.

Similarly, on a podcast, I chanced upon another prominent author expounding upon prethas and bhutas. But once again, I couldn't shake the feeling that this too was being articulated from a Western perspective. While certain concepts overlap in spirit and ancestor worship, it became clear to me, after interviewing experts for my book, that there is no consensus when it comes to certain terminologies. In fact, the concepts change from family to family, village to village, district to district and state to state, across the country. There is a different view of the local scholars which may contradict with those who are practicing the rituals. As seeker of all things existential and beyond, I think it is my duty to explore the true nature of these ethereal elements from an objective point of view, and not be swayed by bias, but it remains essential to classify spirits subjectively, at least for the span of this book.

Where do spirits come from? Do they live in our world? Do they live in another realm? Is this spirit realm coexisting in ours or on another dimension? To understand the concept of the spirit realm, we must probe deeper into the intricate world of Indian lore and spirituality. As I do so, my mind is consumed by contemplation of the definition and etymology of the diverse terminologies that encompass the realm of spirits and deities. Each word bears a wealth of significance, steeped in a unique history in different regions of our country that intricately interweaves with the rich fabric of the broader 'Indian culture' that is perceived by the outside world. And yet, as I ponder over their profound implications, I am humbled by the realization that my understanding remains a work in progress, constantly evolving as I unravel new layers of complexity, results of which you will find in my future works in this genre. This pursuit of knowledge is an unrelenting journey, an endless quest to fathom the nuances of a culture that I was born into, an event on which I had no control upon. In fact, the journey of a spirit into the womb of a mother is explained in different ways. As I traverse the depths of Indian lore and spirituality, I am awed by the profound impact that these concepts have had on the lives of countless people throughout history. Despite the diversity, the truth hides behind the veils of life (birth), death and consciousness.

The perspective that considers the body as fundamental and equates consciousness with the physical form is indeed a simplistic and common viewpoint on human existence. This perspective often simplifies the complexities of life and death, providing a straightforward understanding that aligns with materialistic beliefs. However, in cultures where consciousness holds a more profound significance, the concept of death is perceived as merely the initiation of a potentially infinite cycle. At times, I ponder which is more primitive—the imagination of a person who believes that living beings become spirits after death, or the absolute denial of the spiritual existence after death by a rationalist.

In the Hindu scheme of things, the concept of death, referred to as dehanta, is rooted in the amalgamation of two terms, 'deha' and 'anta,' which literally translates to 'the end of the body'. At the moment of death, something departs the deha, signifying the soul or spirit, comprising only vayu (air) and aakasha (ether). Whether this soul encapsulates consciousness or if it's the other way around is another debate. After this, the performance of proper funeral rites become imperative to facilitate the ascent of the departed soul to pitr-loka.

In 1901, Dr. Duncan McDougall, an American physician, started working on a distinctive experiment with the intent of unraveling the weight of the human soul. His methodology involved a meticulous measurement of the body weight of six patients before and after their demise. The unfolding narrative revealed intriguing findings, suggesting that the soul carries a weight of twenty-one grams. This deduction stemmed from the averaged body weight difference observed in patient subjects mere moments after the cessation of life. Although it was dismissed later as this phenomenon could be attributed to the air leaving the lungs and the sweat produced at the time of death. Nevertheless, the hypothesis opens a speculative avenue. It prompts contemplation on whether the air or vayu, hypothetically constituting the spirit, aligns with the preta form that departs the body in various cultural interpretations of the afterlife.

In the Garuda Purana, it is mentioned that the one who doesn't obtain antyeshti is condemned to wander eternally as a 'preta' (pretha if you are from the south). Antyeshti is composed of the words antya and ishti, which respectively mean 'last' and 'sacrifice'. Together, the word means the 'last sacrifice'. It is also commonly referred to as *antima sanskaara, kriya karm*, etc. As the traditional religions of India are based on the belief in rebirth, pretas, therefore, are destined to suffer as incorporeal spirits in the afterlife because of their insatiable hunger and thirst. Sometimes they cause harm to humans. The concept of pretas and their potential to cause harm to humans shares similarities with the widespread global belief in ghosts. In various cultures worldwide, there is a shared understanding of incorporeal spirits that may haunt people or places after death. Many a times, preta and bhuta are used interchangeably.

Let us now turn our attention to bhuta, a term that refers to the 'past' or 'something that existed in the past'. In our popular culture and literature, the bhuta is a supernatural entity, often described as the ghost of a deceased person. The nuances of how bhutas come into existence vary depending on the region and community, but what is common among them all is that these spirits are often perturbed and restless, unable to move on to their next life. This inability to move on may be due to a violent death, unresolved issues in their past lives, or even improper funeral rites performed by their survivors.

It is interesting to note that bhuta has different connotations in various texts. For instance, in the *Shivapurana*, bhuta refers to the five 'elements', while in the *Natyashastra*, they are assigned as protectors of the natyamandapa or the stage where dance is to take place. When Brahma visited the natyamandapa constructed by Viswakarma, he assigned bhutas to protect these parts from envious malevolent spirits. These bhutas are worshipped before the rangapuja, and their masks must be represented with long hair. In Jain scriptures, bhutas belong to the vyantara class of gods (devas), comprising eight groups of deities that roam the three worlds. The bhutas may also refer to Shiva's attendants in Kailasa that are part of the bhutaganas.

It is worth noting that in the world of Tuluvas, bhutas are not always malevolent spirits, but rather protective spirits and deities. The definition of bhuta within the context of this book derives from the fact that bhuta kola is a dance form, where the paaddanas sometimes invoke Shiva. This dance form originates from a land that was once ruled by Jains, adding another layer of complexity and intrigue to the history and cultural significance of the bhuta. In Tulu Nadu, all communities place great faith in bhutas. When any calamity or misfortune befalls a family, propitiating the bhutas is considered essential. The worship of bhutas has evolved over time, blending elements of both primitive and Puranic propitiation.

Daivas

The word daiva in Sanskrit means relating to gods, caused by or coming from gods, divine, or celestial. According to some scholars and experts, daivas are those spirits which have originated from a divine source or from prakriti (primordial creative force). There is a rigid hierarchy within the pool of daivas as well. The term daiva or daivangalu is usually applied to those (spirit deities) of higher order that do not partake in animal food (Gowda, 2005, pg. no. 20). This distinction may have originated from the influence of Brahminism and Jainism, both of which advocate vegetarianism. In contrast, some bhutas may accept non-vegetarian and liquor offerings.

Though many people use the term daiva and bhuta interchangeably, but some believers perceive bhuta as a derogatory term due to its potential association with malevolent ghosts as well as spirits that are considered tutelary. While certain terms and concepts overlap in spirit worship, it is essential to understand and appreciate the nuances and diversity of Indian beliefs and practices. For most part of this book, I will respectfully employ the term 'daiva', while in English, 'spirit deities', rather than the previously prevalent usage of 'tutelary deities'.

Naagas

I think it would be wrong to not mention naagas in this section as they are also considered divine beings in Tulu Nadu and Kerala. Naagas are highly respected due to the belief that Parashurama forged a covenant with Naagaraja Vasuki while banishing the serpents from the emerging landmass. Often people translate naaga aaradhane as snake worship, but the more respectable term would be serpent worship. Serpent deities are the chthonic deities that are believed to grant fertility as well as affect physical and mental wellbeing of an individual and her family members. Every family has a naagabana or serpent grove in Tulu Nadu. In Kerala, such groves are called sarpa kaavus. Some people do not shy away from including naagadaivas into the fold of 'satyolu' that are worshipped in the region.

Bermer

Bermer is considered the highest among the daivas, and perhaps the oldest. Some people associate Bermer with Naaga-Brahma and even the Puranic Brahma. It is essential to note, however, that many say that Bermer is distinct from Lord Brahma of the Hindu trinity or the myth of Brahmarakshas. In some regions, Bermer has perhaps merged into a form of Shiva, known as Brahmalingeshwara or Shaasta. Bermer is also established in the garadis, where he is commonly represented in the form of a mustachioed warrior. He is often portrayed with a sword in one hand and straddling astride on a horse. This form bears an uncanny resemblance to Lord Ayyappa, the deity worshipped in Kerala. Although Ayyappa is generally depicted seated on a tiger carrying a bow in paintings, the vaji vahana or the horse vehicle is visible on the kodimaram (flagstaff) at Sabarimala. Interestingly, Ayyappa is also known as Dharma Shaasta and Bhutanaatha (Lord of all bhutas) among his devotees in Kerala. There is another beautiful story of two Kenjava birds that appear at the beginning of time. According to this story, one of their eggs falls on earth. From the broken shell emerged two majestic palaces. It is there that a divine child was born who went on to become Bermer. It would not be amiss to speculate that Bermer may have been a warrior deity of ancient times, and through fusion with other religious beliefs and influence, the original identity has been lost. In the story of Siri, there are multiple mentions of Bermer. In fact, the story begins with the arrival of Bermer in the form of a Brahmin. Similarly, in Koti Chennaya's epic, the warrior brothers are shown as worshipping Naagabrahma.

It is believed that Bermer was born according to shastras when the earth was created. There were seven types of Gangas, a rough translation for rivers or seas. In the middle of the seventh Ganga, the Surya Narayana or the personification of sun came into existence. He emerges with Bermer on his back. I was fortunate enough to be able to attend one kola of Bermer in Shishila during my stay last summer. There are a lot of conflicting views on the origin and identity of Bermer and it is difficult to give one concrete answer. However, it is agreed upon that Bermer or Bermeru is the most important deity among the daivas.

5

The Origin of Bhutas

IN THE INDIAN TRADITION, THE STORY OF CREATION is multifaceted and intricate. As with many myths, there are several versions of this tale, each with their own nuances and particularities. Some versions speak of a vast primordial ocean in which a golden egg appeared, containing within it the seed of Brahma, the creator of the universe. In other accounts, Adi Narayana, the primeval and eternal source of all things, is depicted as sleeping on infinite waters at the beginning of time. Whereas in Shiva-centred stories, Brahma is born out of Mahadeva. In the Devi Bhagavata Purana, it is recounted that at the end of the kalpa (age), Vishnu cluelessly pondered upon his own birth while lying as a baby on a banyan leaf floating on the endless primordial ocean. In response to his musings, the Devi Bhagavati proclaimed through a celestial voice that everything seen is her own manifestation. Thus, taking place of the all pervading consciousness or Supreme Being. Despite these variations, one constant runs through all the versions of the story: the recognition that Brahma is not the ultimate or primordial creator but rather emerges from a deeper, more all-encompassing power known as 'Brahman'. Many of you may have heard this terminology before. For those hearing it for the first time, please note that it is not pronounced as 'braah-min,' which refers to the priestly caste. Brahman or the all-encompassing super consciousness is pronounced as 'brahm-man'. This ineffable and transcendent force pervades all cycles of creation and destruction, sustaining and guiding it at every moment. It is the manifestation beyond the limits of the simulation of 'Maya'.

In his publication, 'The Origin of the Demons', Rev Manner presents a paaddana that explores the descent of the spirit deities. Please note that though the title says 'Origin of the Bhutas' but this story doesn't delve into the actual genesis of the bhutas. However, I have recounted an intriguing origin tale from a 10th-century Kashmiri manuscript in the section following this story. As previously discussed, within this framework, the Tulu daivas are perceived as the attendant ganas of Shiva. There is speculation among scholars that this portrayal of daivas as bhutaganas may have been influenced by Shaivism. In the subsequent passages, I have taken the liberty to creatively expound upon the lore in the form of a story.

The Story

As Lord Narayana surveyed the creation of bhuloka, the earth, he was flanked on either side by the great deities Shiva and Brahma. The holy trinity gazed down upon their handiwork with pride from their celestial abode.

Ishvara, or Shiva, spoke with admiration, 'Look at this marvel—you have created a breathtaking array of eight million and forty thousand living species. From the intelligent humans to the majestic mammals, the soaring birds and the crawling reptiles, all the way down to the tiniest of ants and insects. And you have provided for them all, with proper food and sustenance. You have appointed great rulers in every direction of the compass—Indra, Agni, Yama, Neiretye, Varun, Vayu, Kubera, and Isanya. And to govern the passing of time, you have placed two great bodies in the sky—the radiant sun and the serene moon. And in your generosity, you have bestowed upon them six seasons of moist rain and six seasons of dryness. We are overjoyed with what you have created.'

With a serene smile on his face, Lord Narayana replied, 'Indeed, you and I, along with Brahma, as the trinity, must take control of both bhuloka and paraloka. We shall be known henceforth as Brahma, Vishnu and Maheshwara. My task shall be to maintain, Brahma shall create, and Maheshwara shall bring about the great destruction of pralaya at the end of times.'

With great devotion and skill, they set about their tasks, each carving out a domain that would serve as their abode. Narayana, the great preserver, settled himself in Vaikuntha, while Ishvara chose to make his home in the icy peaks of Kailasa. Brahma, on the other hand, established his base in Satyaloka, from where he embarked on his great project of creation.

The devaloka, consisting of three hundred thirty million gods (thirty-three koti), was his greatest accomplishment. This celestial realm was inhabited by an array of beings—demigods, sages, seers, celestial beings and muses—all of whom were presided over by the great Devendra.

All seemed well in the universe, and the gods rejoiced in the beauty of their creation. But one day, while sitting with his wife Parvati in the presence of Veerabhadra, his one thousand one ganas, and one thousand one bhutas, Ishvara was asked a question.

Parvati, known for her insatiable curiosity and thirst for knowledge, inquired of her husband, 'Oh Ishvara, the people that you have created do not always live a pious life. Some of them commit sins. If not checked, the sinners will keep increasing. Tell me, what fate awaits those who commit sins?'

Ishvara, with a tender and compassionate gaze, looked at his wife and replied, 'My dearest Parvati, the answer to your question lies all around us.'

Parvati looked around at the ganas and bhutas on either side of Ishvara, waiting for him to continue.

'These beings have served me with great devotion and loyalty,' Ishvara continued. 'In recognition of their service, I created a thousand and one diseases that afflict the earth.'

Parvati was taken aback by this revelation. 'For whom?' she asked.

'For those people on earth, who forget to lead a pious life. Those people on earth who become greedy for wealth and power. For those people on earth who forget the blood in their veins is one.'

'What happens when the number of such wicked, money-loving, proud sinners increase on earth?' she asked.

'The pride of the people on earth would increase, and such people will oppress the poor and the less fortunate. So, in order to punish such sinners, I did as I did. At that time all these bhutas assembled and prostrated before me. They said they suffered hunger and thirst, and that they could not contain it any longer. When they thus requested, I instructed them to descend to earth and give trouble to sinners. When these people realize what's troubling them then they will give food to the bhutas from their hands and promise to mend their ways. Shiva particularly reminds the bhutas not to trouble those who lead a pious life.'

Parvati was amused upon learning this; however, Ishvara wasn't done yet, for there was more to the story. He recollected, 'When I instructed the bhutas to go after sinners on earth, they had a valid question as to how they would identify who is a sinner and who is not?'

'What did you say?'

'I told them that I shall beforehand send the sinners troubles. The bhutas can then find such persons and get food from them. Then the bhutas had another dilemma.'

'What was that?'

'How could those suffering under the grasp of such entities, possibly realize their plight? Furthermore, how might those who have committed sinful acts know to offer appeasement to these otherworldly beings? I responded to their quandary by reminding them that those stricken with iniquity would be directed by mediums knowledgeable in the ways of astrology, sorcery and other oracular arts. Yet, the bhutas yearned for further insight, inquiring as to their earthly destination. They wanted to know where they will go on earth. Thus, I told them I would allot them different names and they should go to the Southern kingdoms to settle down. Additionally, I assured them that more of their kindred would be dispatched in the days to come. At last, the bhutas were content, and took their leave, while the deities Mahakali, Veerabhadra and Mari appeared before me, eyes ablaze like fiery coals.'

'What did they say?'

'They asked me if I had forgotten them as they also want to be shown a way to receive food and offerings from people. So, I told them that Dhumavathi is in Mudabidri. I told them to show their power to the people from that place to the sea in the west, and receive kolas and other offerings from the people. Thus, they were also dismissed and I sent away all of them to earth to take food and offerings from people, and to keep a check on sinners.'

Thus, it was believed that bhutas descended to the earth to watch over and protect the devout while keeping a close eye on the errant sinners. This origin story is rooted in the notion that the bhuta cult of the region was assimilated into the larger Hindu religious framework. It is intriguing to observe the vastness of the Hindu pantheon depicted in this paaddana. The term 'thirty-three koti' is utilized, typically interpreted as 'thirty-three crores' or 'three hundred thirty million' gods. However, the Sanskrit term 'koti' carries another connotation, denoting 'category' or 'class.' Traayastrimsha, or the heaven of thirty-three gods is an important concept in Buddhism as well. Thus, the frequently misunderstood count may actually signify thirty-three distinct classes or categories of gods and deities. In the Brihadaranyaka Upanishad, it is mentioned that the hundreds of gods are manifestations of the thirty-three gods. The eight Vasus, the eleven Rudras, and the twelve Adityas constitute thirty-one, and Indra and Prajapati complete the thirty-three. Within the Hindu pantheon, Shiva or Ishvara is referred to as Bhutanatha or the divine Lord of the bhutas. According to P. Padmanabha's 'Special Study Report on Bhuta Cult in South Kanara District', this may be how the pre-existing practice of spirit veneration was eventually supplanted under the auspices of Ishvara.

The Origin of Bhutas in a Shaivite Text

The narrative above delves not into the genesis of the bhutas, but rather details their descent to earth and the purpose behind it. A fascinating parallel can be drawn from an ancient Shaivite text originating from Kashmir, which portrays Parvati's query to Shiva regarding afflictions and the evil eye. Shiva, in response, unravels the origin of the Bhutas.

As per this rendition, when the daityas prevailed over the devas, Indra sought aid from Shiva. After assuming the formidable form of Svachandabhairava, Shiva fashioned potent entities known as the bhutas, the grahas, and the maatars (mother goddesses). Their purpose was to defeat the malevolent daityas and restore the dominion of the devas. Upon achieving this feat, Shiva bestowed upon these supernatural entities the gift of invincibility (ajeya).

Types of Spirit Deities

Rev Manner had previously categorized the spirits of Tulu Nadu into fifteen distinct groups. However, contemporary scholars have now refined this classification system, and the spirit deities of Tulu Nadu are now commonly divided into the subsequent categories:

1. Totemistic spirits
2. Puranic deities
3. Martyr spirits
4. Spirits of diverse origin

Totemistic Spirits

Totemism is a belief system that posits a mystical relationship between human beings and spirit-beings, such as animals or plants. In fact, Totemism predates almost all forms of religions. Entities known as totems are believed to interact with individuals or kin groups, serving as their symbols or emblems. Totemism is a complex concept that encompasses a range of ideas and behaviors rooted in a worldview drawn from nature. This includes ideological, mystical, emotional, reverential and genealogical relationships between social groups or individuals and animals or natural objects—the totems. In the olden times, humans gave meaning to their lives through totemistic rituals.

Pilichandi, Nandigone, Naaga, Mahisandaye, and now popularized by *Kantara*—Panjurli, are some of the totemistic spirits who originate from tiger (pili), bull (nandi), buffalo (mahisha), serpent (naaga) and boar (panji). Primitive religions and magic hold wild animals of the forests, seas and skies in high regard. These early human cultures, grounded in the practice of hunting and gathering, understood that taking the life of an animal not only provided sustenance and raw materials, but also risked incurring the wrath of its ruling spirit. In response, villagers who fell prey to the bite of a poisonous snake or whose crops were destroyed by wild boars sought to appease the governing spirit of the offending animal. It was this fascination with and observation of the natural world that birthed animal worship in primitive man. For instance, Pilichandi is believed to save cattle from getting taken by tigers. What started as curiosity over unique animal traits gradually evolved into profound reverence and adoration, a belief in the sacredness of certain creatures that often results in the imposition of dietary laws prohibiting their consumption.

Puranic Spirits

The Puranic spirits, originating from Hindu Puranas, are revered as spirit deities embodying various entities such as the avatars of Shiva, Vishnu, or Shakti, as well as the attendants (ganas) of Shiva. This is exemplified by the story of how Shiva dispatched attendants from Kailasa to the earthly realm, as stated in the preceding section. Take, for example, Veerabhadra, an attendant gana of Shiva.

On the Vaishnava side, there is Vishnumurthy, embodying Narasimha. Vishnumurthy's 'otte-kola' is performed in the southern parts of Tulu Nadu like Sulya, Puttur, and Kasaragod (Kerala). Further south, Vishnumurthy becomes a significant deity in theyyam rituals of North Kerala and is known for its agnipravesha.

Spirit deities like Jumaadi, Lakkesiri, and Maari are believed to be incarnations of the mother goddess. However, some scholars contest this, arguing that the inclusion of Puranic deities occurred later with the diffusion of Brahminical influence, linking native spirits to the Puranic gods and mother goddesses. Quoting from an article, 'The powerful Maariamma is the bhootha of the epidemics described as the small-pox goddess of south India in the 1971 census report. Most traditions involving Maariamma reaffirm the belief that she is a bhootha. But newer traditions involving the deity have reinterpreted her as Shakti or an incarnation of Goddess Durga.' (The News Minute, 22 March 2022).

Martyr Spirits

In various cultures worldwide, a martyr is an individual who has died tragically for a noble cause, while apotheosis refers to the deification of such a hero. However, in our culture, the belief that death is not the end of everything makes this concept acceptable and particularly widespread. The spirit lives after death and even takes rebirth. Local heroes and royal figures are often deified to the point that they may have merged with the Puranic gods. In Tulu Nadu, for instance, Koti and Chennaya became divine figures after their heroic demise. They are now martial deities who are worshipped in designated places known as garodi or garadi.

Spirits of Diverse Origin

In addition to the Puranic spirits, there are other entities in Hindu belief that are revered and propitiated. Among these are the spirits of humans who suffered a tragic death, such as Koraga-Taniya, affectionately known as Koragajja, as well as Kordabbu and Tannimaaniga. These individuals had a connection with the daivas, and in death, they transformed into spirits themselves. Others, like Kodamanithaaya and Jaarandaaya, are known as rajandaiyolu or royal spirits, while some spirits are considered joruda or ferocious, such as Guliga and Chaundi.

Food for Thought

When exploring tales of gods, spirits and folk deities, one encounters a myriad of versions. There's the rendition embraced by the common folk, another espoused by religious authorities to propagate the faith, and yet another, the academic and anthropological perspective, which may diverge from popular beliefs. Consequently, discerning the truth amidst these varied narratives poses a formidable challenge.

Essentially, as religion or culture evolves, it assimilates and melds with preexisting beliefs, eventually becoming inseparable and indiscernible. Initially, there may have been a primitive folk religion that varied from one human settlement to another. It's possible that the revered deities were once completely detached from the Puranic influence of today.

Another theory to contemplate is the notion that some of these spirit deities might have originated from the Puranic gods and mother goddesses. This raises the possibility that these deities were known and depicted differently in various geographic regions. However, as information travelled and cultures interacted, people began to identify commonalities among these spirits. Over time, these diverse entities may have been assimilated under a broader conceptual umbrella—a process that is still ongoing until we uncover the truth... the Satya.

Having said that, recognizing commonalities among diverse folk deities from different regions doesn't erase their unique characteristics. Just as different shades of red share the essence of 'redness' yet possess distinct qualities, these spirit deities might share certain underlying themes or functions while retaining their individual identities and nuances. This distinction is crucial, unlike mistaking entirely different colours like blue and red.

6

The Sacred Realm

THE CACOPHONOUS CITY LIFE IS ENOUGH TO drive anyone mad, but seeking refuge in a remote hamlet can be a surreal experience. I remember one such episode from my recent past that still sends shivers down my spine; an encounter with a mysterious presence that was beyond my wildest imagination. It was a small village in Karkala, where I had taken up residence in my relative's ancestral house, a century-old structure standing in isolation, several hundred metres away from any other dwelling. The atmosphere was eerily quiet, a stark contrast to the urban hubbub that I was used to. As a writer of horror, I could sense the perfect milieu in which I found myself, but nothing could have prepared me for the terrifying events that were about to unfold.

I had a fitful night's sleep on my first night in the house, resting outdoors, right outside the chavadi with other guests who had come to attend a ceremony the next morning. The sky rumbled with distant thunder, and a gentle breeze swept over me. In the midst of this, I had a bizarre dream in which I was walking outside when a disembodied hand appeared, pointing insistently in one direction. A red fire also glowed on the ground around me. There was a narrow opening that was leading somewhere. The red flames were trying to provoke me to take the path. Upon waking, these were the only detail that remained vivid in my memory. The next day, a lengthy ceremonial ritual kept me occupied for half the day, leaving me exhausted in the searing heat of April. Later, I found myself outdoors once again with several other guests, reclining outside the chavadi. As I drifted off into a restless slumber, I was suddenly jolted awake by an inexplicable sense of dread, as though an ominous presence lurked just behind me. I could not summon the courage to turn around, gripped by an unshakeable terror that persisted throughout the night; a kind of dread that I had never felt in life. Whether it was a vivid nightmare or a bout of sleep paralysis, I could not be certain. Despite closing my eyes in an attempt to escape the dread, sleep eluded me. Eventually, I sensed something brushing against me, prompting me to open my eyes. There was a striking black cat perched at the window, its emerald eyes fixed upon mine. Strangely, its presence offered a sense of reassurance, coinciding with the gradual fading of the eerie presence that had loomed behind me.

The next morning, I recounted my unsettling experiences to my relative. I mentioned the dream I had had of the hand pointing in a specific direction, and her reaction was one of astonishment. She informed me that the sthaana of the area's protective spirit deity was located precisely in that direction. Without hesitation, she led me to the sthaana, where I offered my prayers to the Chamundi residing therein. From that moment on, my stay in the house was free from any scary encounters.

While explaining this to a friend of mine who knows a thing or two about psychology, he suggested that the human mind persistently seeks out patterns and connections in the world around us. This confirmation bias is the innate inclination to search for information that affirms our preexisting beliefs. However, in unfamiliar or unsettling environments, such as a remote village at night, our minds may wander into the realm of the supernatural, seeking out patterns or connections that suggest the existence of otherworldly beings. The instinctual fight or flight response, triggered by a sense of dread or a perceived threat, further exacerbates these experiences. The amalgamation of the confirmation bias and the fight or flight response can create eerie, spine-chilling events, even in the absence of a supernatural explanation. Seeking solace, such as visiting a religious site and offering prayers, can provide a semblance of comfort and closure in such situations.

Nevertheless, a year later, as I returned to the same house while researching for this very book that you are now reading, I felt a familiar chill run down my spine one night. But this time, I was armed with the knowledge of the sthaana's existence. I offered my prayers without fail. And while I slept peacefully throughout my stay, the memory of that eerie night still haunts me. For in the world of horror and folklore, the line between reality and imagination is often blurred, and the inexplicable can turn out to be far more terrifying than any fiction.

Where Daivas Are Worshipped

At the centre of a typical Tulu household, whether grand or modest, lies the kone or chamber where the family deities are revered. In some houses, like my spouse's ancestral house, a large wooden plank that hangs from the ceiling is used as a swinging cot for the spirit deities. All the objects that pertain to the spirit deity are present in this chamber. When it comes to community worship, this could also be in the form of a small hut or a modern concrete structure situated somewhere in the village. This is referred to as a sthaana (or saana or bhutasthaana). At times, it may even be situated within the temple premise. The annual festival of kola or nema takes place at the sthaana or a short distance away from it, where devotees offer their homage to the spirit deities. Since some (or most) of the bhutas are referred to as daivas, their sthaanas are also called daiva-sthaana. For a non-Tulu reader, this may sound like 'deva-sthaana' but it is not the same. You see, devasthana is the term used for temples of Puranic gods like Vishnu or Ishvara. The word deva and daiva are not used interchangeably here as both mean different entities. The spaces dedicated to beidarlu is called garadi. Gudi is another place dedicated to the spirit deities. Siris are worshipped in Alades.

Bhandaara

Another important aspect of the physical realm are the objects issued to the spirit deities. The idol, ghante or a hand bell, the mugga (mask), kadsale (a type of sword), shields, chowries (which is a bushy fan made out of yak's hair), goblet and weapons pertaining to the spirit deity are the important paraphernalia which are often placed in the kone, bhandara mane or sthaana. These sacred objects of the spirit deity are collectively referred to as bhandaara.

The World of Spirits

During an online speaking engagement with a group of readers of *Dakhma*, a curious voice chimed with an intriguing question: 'Where do spirits come from when they are not possessing people?' I must confess, such a query had crossed my mind on numerous occasions. So, let us in a broader context, ponder on a crucial inquiry: where do spirits reside when they are not invoked?

In search of an answer, we must explore two essential and universal concepts of existence—the tangible and the intangible. The former is entrenched in the physical reality that is perceivable by humans. It could manifest in the form of idols, objects of the spirits, or even humans (when possessed).

But in the incident that I recollected at the start of this chapter, if there indeed was a spirit behind me that night at my relative's house, then where did it come from? Is it a metaphysical manifestation or simply an illusion? So, allow me, dear reader, to delve deeper into the esoteric concepts of the intangible realm of spirits, an elusive world that may be believed to hover all around us, omnipresent yet unseen and unproven by science (yet). In many cultures, it is believed that spirits come from the spirit world, while others claim that they are present all around us.

In the mystical worship of daivas, a tangible form of reality may be the physical world that we inhabit. According to beliefs, spirits in their tangible form may even reside in rocks that are placed under trees. However, most commonly, the idols and paraphernalia of spirit deities are found in a chamber inside the house or at sthaanas. Then there is a sacred realm, where spirits and supernatural entities of various spiritual manifestations may be believed to reside, whether they be benevolent or malevolent. The notion of a spirit realm can be found in almost every culture and it has trickled down to the modern times as well. However, unlike the western notion of the spirit realm as an external environment for spirits, the spirit world in this context might be considered to be in concentric existence with the physical world.

In a generic invocation performed during the ritual, the spirit deity is invoked to descend from the aakasha, symbolizing the ethereal realm beyond the skies, into the earthly realm, denoting the material plane or physical dimension. Subsequently, the deity is beseeched to enter the designated sacred space, known as the sthaana, and then to inhabit the cot where the idol is positioned. Then in the final part conjures the spirit into the body of a 'child' birthed by a mother, poetically referring to a 'man'—in this context, the dancer eagerly anticipating possession by the spirit deity.

In the tangible material world, spirits are afforded a physical dwelling in sthaanas, a place where they are revered and offered veneration. As mentioned before, these sthaanas can take the form of a small hut, a modern concrete structure, or even a temple premise. However, the true essence of the spirit realm is intangible in nature and beyond the limits of human perception with the five senses. Through the mediumship at the time of a kola or nema, the spirit deity from this elusive realm is believed to join (joga/yog) the physical body (or loukika shareera) of the medium, and communicate with the physical world. There are two types of human mediums in spirit worship of Tulu Nadu; the kola dancer and darshanapatri oracle. Any ordinary person cannot be possessed by the spirit deity. According to the customs and beliefs of the people, the medium must belong to the particular community that is allowed to impersonate the spirit, and more importantly, he must adhere to strict rules and discipline before possession. They consider the body of the medium as a house for the spirit to stay while it is on earth.

The belief in the existence of a spirit realm is not limited to a single belief system. It is a feature of folks stories in many parts of the world. This universality of certain cognitive traits and abilities, which results in supernatural beliefs such as animism, the apotheosis of heroes, and the faith in a spirit world, could potentially be rooted in the evolutionary process that early humans underwent as they adapted to their surroundings and overcame challenges. As time passed, certain advantageous cognitive traits and abilities may have become widespread throughout the human population, leading to a certain degree of commonality in human thinking across various cultures and geographies. However, it is essential to acknowledge that cultural and environmental factors also played a substantial role in shaping the distinct beliefs, values and practices of different human societies.

Coming back to the sacred realm of the spirit deities, what enthralls me most is the etymology of the term 'maya'. In the Tulu language, 'maaju poppuna' connotes fading away or to vanish. Quite close to its Malayalam counterpart 'maanju pokuka' or 'maayavaagu' in Kannada. This concept might be rooted in the word maya, which means trickery, or illusion, which signifies some form of magic. To illustrate, when you erase something written on a paper, the content disappears. This, in essence, is maya. The same word is employed to imply an illusion in the metaphysical notions of Indic religions. According to local folklore, performers in the olden days were said to disappear into Maya at the peak of their performance. In cases of some spirit deities, when they were human and wronged, they were believed to have disappeared from earth and turned into a spirit. Erase, fade, disappear, vanish, illusion, magic—all these words are synonymous with maya.

The Reality of the Surreal World of the Spirits

What if, in the world we inhabit, there exists a realm beyond our limited perception—a domain where spirits of various kinds dwell? Here, one might encounter the daivas, the bhutas, the ganas, the maatrs, the grahas, minor supernatural entities, and even the restless pretas. The notion that these otherworldly beings, both benevolent and malevolent, roam amongst us unseen is a deeply rooted belief. It is a belief that holds sway over the people of Tulu Nadu as well, a belief that is as old as time itself. In some cultures, even omens are considered as invisible supernatural creatures that live in hamlets and forests, in waters, in land, in the sky, moving by day or by night or by both day and night (Iyer, 1884, p. 177). Our folklores are full of omens, both good and bad, that shape the narrative for generations to follow. There are primarily two kinds of invisible entities all around us; those that crawl on the land and then those who fly in the air. As per such folklores, there are minor supernatural beings that are believed to affect the daily lives of people by causing diseases, casting evil eyes, bringing bad luck, etc. Such supernatural beings are pleased at the sight of coconuts cracking during a traditional coconut fight. Now, imagine a world that you, as a human, cannot witness, but exists all around with such sinister creatures. That's scary, I'd say. The daiva, according to folk beliefs, who reigns supreme in this mystical realm, is believed to protect people of the village from the malefic mischiefs of such beings.

As we delve deeper into this supernatural realm, we come to realize that, akin to the Puranic Naagaloka, it is a place that is beyond the human imagination. Those who do not believe in spirits may view it as nothing more than fanciful fiction fueled by extreme devotion, which is absolutely fine and rationally acceptable. The easiest way to live this life is by accepting only what you see and what can be proved, and that everything ends with physical demise. Scientific temperament can only acknowledge consciousness as the brain's trickery to keep you pumping thanklessly till the inevitable end. The nature of consciousness remains a complex and multidimensional topic, and different scientific, philosophical, and religious perspectives exist. Many argue for a materialistic explanation, while others propose dualistic or panpsychist views, suggesting a deeper and possibly non-physical aspect to consciousness.

Nevertheless, the fact remains that there are many mysteries in this world that we have yet to unravel. Perhaps the sacred realm of spirits and spirit deities is one such mystery that may be connected with some form of collective consciousness that we are not aware of right now. It is a world that we may never be able to discover or comprehend, a world that is shrouded in the unknown. It could also be the invention of a creative mind's escapism. The things that we know are finite, the things we don't know are infinite. It is this infinite nature of this world that makes it such a fascinating and wondrous place. Who knows what lies beyond the veil that separates our physical realm from the sacred realm of spirits? Perhaps it is a place of great beauty and wonder, or perhaps it is just this world that exists everywhere.

7

The Ritualistic Dance

THE DIVINE DANCES OF THE SPIRIT DEITIES, expressed in kola, is an integral part of Tulu Nadu's culture. The kola occurs periodically to honour the spirit deities. The word 'kola' is derived from the Tulu language and means 'decoration' or 'beautiful attire,' which reflects the stunning colours of the makeup, clothes, and headgear worn by the performers. The nema, on the other hand, is believed to originate from the word 'niyama,' which means a set of rules or principles that are followed. Another intriguing feature of the region's temples is the ratha (theru/chariot) utsava. In a similar manner, rajan daivas (kingly or royal spirit deities) are paraded around the temple in a vehicle or chariot, which is called bandi (d is pronounced as in doctor). The date for kola is either decided in consultation with an astrologer or it takes place on a fixed day every year. During my stay last summer in Tulu Nadu, I traversed past numerous banners and signboards announcing nema or kola celebrations on my way from Karkala to Mangalore. Most of these traditional celebrations that have been a part of Tulu Nadu's cultural heritage for ages are primarily held between December and May, when the skies are clear and the monsoons are yet to arrive. As the weather turns humid and moist from June onwards, the locals prepare themselves for the onset of the rainy season.

Tulu Nadu, with its tropical monsoon climate, experiences heavy rainfall from June to September and relatively dry conditions from December to February. The region's annual precipitation measures around 3,000 millimeters, providing a nurturing environment for the local flora and fauna. The temperature in Tulu Nadu remains moderate for most of the year, ranging from 20 to 36 degrees Celsius, with occasional high temperatures during the summer months. However, due to the humidity and the global rise in temperature, summer months have become unbearable in recent times. Indeed, I happened to be there during Christmas last year, and, if I may express, the warmth was quite palpable, leading to a rather unexpected bout of sweating. The credit can also go to the rampant deforestation paving way for developmental activities.

In the month of Aati (July-August), when the rain gods are most exuberant, no ceremonial events are supposed to take place. A similar belief is held in neighbouring Kerala, where people retreat indoors and recite verses from the Ramayana during the same month which is known as Karkidakam in Malayalam. In Tulu region, a unique kind of performance takes place during Aati known as 'Aati Kalenja'. Members of the Nalike community don vibrant costumes and go from house to house as Kalinja. In exchange for their performance, people offer rice, vegetables and money to the artists. It is believed that during the month of Aati, the spirit of nature, Kalenja, descends upon the earth to bestow blessings upon the land and its people. Since the monsoon season is notorious for spreading infectious diseases, Aati Kalenja is thought to ward off the evil spirits that cause such afflictions (*Deccan Herald*, 2015).

Furthermore, the region also practices 'kaalakola', wherein the spirits of recently departed family members are summoned. This ritual takes place on the sixteenth day following the person's passing. The 'Jaalatta' is also a type of ritualistic dance where multiple spirits are invoked into the bodies of dancers from the Nalike community. Although rare, this one doesn't have any Puranic deities involved and some scholars believe this to be spirit veneration closer to its original form. It is intriguing to consider the role that these spirits and spirit deities play in the lives of the people of Tulu Nadu. Their beliefs in these rituals are deeply rooted, and their devotion is unwavering, perhaps due to the tangible effects that such practices have on their lives.

During bygone eras, it was customary for performing artists to reside on the same property as the landlords, and only those artists who belonged to a particular region were permitted to perform the kola ritual for the daivas. Equally essential were the other participants, including the mediator and musicians, who were also required to reside within the region. I was told that each daiva in a given region adhered to peculiar traditions specific to that area, which only those acquainted with it would be able to comprehend. Nonetheless, in recent times, due to the implications of circumstances arising from the modern way of life, this practice has been diluted in many locales.

Nevertheless, the enduring practice of kola and daiva aaradhane, persisting through ages of cultural and political transformations, stands as a testament to the resilience of Tulu Nadu's heritage. Its survival in its present form is truly commendable, especially when similar practices have faded away in other cultures. Yes, there are debates on whether classical songs or film songs should be played during the performance, but those are truly trivial matters.

The important thing is that the tradition and the dance form has survived. The credit for preserving these traditions belongs to the Tulu people, spanning all classes and communities, who have safeguarded them through the sands of time. Yes, within the different communities or different generations within the same community, differences may exist, but the unifying force of the daivas appears to transcend these differences. In the complex web of beliefs, rituals and traditions, the daivas emerge as a binding hand that weaves together the varied strands of the society, fostering a sense of shared identity and collective heritage.

8
Steps Involved in Kola

IN THE INTEREST OF PRECISION AND comprehensibility, I'll designate the ritualistic dance as 'kola' and the kola dancer or impersonator as 'artist', in the pages to follow.

Tulu Nadu covers an area of approximately 8,441 square kilometres. The region is bordered by the Western Ghats to the east, and the Arabian Sea to the west. It encompasses the districts of Dakshina Kannada and Udupi in Karnataka state, and Kasaragod in Kerala state. That's almost the distance between Delhi and Mathura or Mumbai and Pune. As we move from north to south of this region, we can note variations in the spoken dialect as well as rituals involved in kola. Thus, the steps intrinsic to a kola may exhibit variances contingent upon both regional peculiarities and the divine entity being evoked. The fundamental nature of this ritualistic performance has been broadly delineated into a set of sixteen distinct steps or 'padinaaji kattu katle' by erudite scholars. 'Padinaaji' is the number 'sixteen,' a figure of unmistakable significance. This perfectly square number occupies a central place in Tulu culture, where it is regarded as an auspicious number. 'Padinaaji panda paripoorna' or sixteen means complete, opines Nellithaya, the esteemed *madhyasthar* or mediator from Puttur, while he explained the importance of the number. This esteem for the 'sixteen' is manifest in a plethora of Tuluva customs, including the mourning period, which extends for a duration of sixteen days, as opposed to the customary thirteen. In some parts, sixteen leaves are placed for sixteen generations of deceased elders. Furthermore, the administrative divisions of Tuluva monarchs were traditionally structured according to multiples of sixteen. (*Indic Today*, 2021).

Regardless of the number of steps involved, beholding a kola in full flow, one can discern the performer undergoing a tripartite metamorphosis, traversing a trio of transformative phases. The idea is that the ritualistic dance progresses through three stages of spiritual metamorphosis. The first stage portrays the aspect of 'youth,' following which the performer dons the 'gaggara,' ushering in the epoch of 'adulthood.' Finally, in the culminating stage, or 'katinema', bedecked with the sacred ornaments of 'ani' and 'mugga,' the artist is believed to attain a state of oneness with the divine spirit. As the narrative unfolds, my reader, you will gain an enhanced comprehension of this profoundly spiritual phenomenon.

A Personal Experience

As the date of kola approaches, the sleepiest of villages buzz with activity and excitement. With expenses to be met, the community comes together to collect contributions. This reminds me of that sultry summer noon when I found myself in the chavadi of Shashi aunty's home, deep in conversation with her and Anasuya dodda about the revered Satyadevathe who was venerated in their house.

After they exchanged stories about the deity, we started talking about the importance of noticing omens in spirit worship. That's when one of Shashi aunty's neighbours joined our gathering, eager to share her own tale about a powerful female deity named Thannimaaniga.

The neighbour had barely begun her story when their rottweiler started barking at the front door. The owner of the house, a middle-aged gentleman, looked confused upon seeing a group of people who had arrived seeking donations for an upcoming kola to be held at a temple in a nearby village. But upon discovering that one of them was a mukkaldi, an officiator who held a special position in the kola ritual, I rushed to meet and talk to him. Those who accompanied him left to visit other houses in the vicinity.

After making a humble contribution to the fund, I asked the mukkaldi if he could enlighten me about the daivas involved in the kola. And to my surprise, one of the main deities was none other than Thannimaaniga (and Kordabbu), the very deity we had just started discussing.

Was that merely a coincidence, or a sign from the spirits themselves?

For the women gathered in that room, the auspiciousness of the timing of the mukkaldi's visit was seen as a blessed omen, which was also a topic of our discussion.

The mukkaldi, who had introduced himself as Kariye, was overjoyed to learn that I was documenting the worship of Tulu Nadu's daivas and happily blessed me for a successful completion. In heartfelt words, he expressed, 'I am so pleased that I shared what I know, and because of you, many more will come to know about our great daivas.'

This encounter left me with a profound sense of awe. I wondered if the spirit deities might be omnipresent like the people believed, silently observing and foreseeing every unfolding plan that eludes our awareness. Did their subtle messages really manifest as omens?

Initial Preparations

In the traditional kola ritual, the members of the Pambada, Parava and Nalike communities are endowed with the duty of performing as artists. In the North Kerala region, the Koppaala and Paanaan are involved in this tradition. Sturrock mentions in the South Canara Manual (Vol. 1) that the Paanaans were the Malayalam caste corresponding to the Nalkes and Pombadas. In Malabar, they were also known by the name Malayan (Sturrock, 1894, pg. no. 180). The Paanaans may have migrated from Tamil Nadu via Palakkad and settled in Paanathur (meaning 'Paanaan's Ooru' or village). From there, they might have migrated to South Canara through Kasaragod (Upadhyaya, 2002, pg. no. 93).

The word Nalike/Nalke means 'dance'. Collectively, they may be known as Nalkedaakul (those who dance) or Kola Kattunaakul (those who adorn the kola). These families were required to reside in the vicinity of the sthaana, and follow strict rules in order to be eligible to perform the ritualistic dance of kola. Once the date for the kola is set, the representative of the organizer extends a customary honorarium of rice and coconut to the artist, signifying the initiation of proceedings (Upadhyaya 2002, p. no. 24). From then on, the artist is bound by strict guidelines and regulations, and must adhere to them stringently. In the event that the artist falls ill, a member of his family is required to take his place. To ensure that the sanctity of the ritual is preserved, the kola artist is prohibited from consuming alcohol and intoxicants, and follows strict dietary restrictions until the completion of the ritual. Such is the discipline and dedication required of those who participate in this time-honoured tradition. There is a hierarchy among these communities as well, and not all of them are allowed to impersonate all the daivas. Another crucial initiation step in the kola ritual is the 'kayil kaduppuna,' or the cutting of the banana bunch.

Banana in South Indian Culture

In Indian culture, the banana holds a significant place in the religious and cultural landscape, featuring prominently in almost every Hindu religious function. As we journey into the southwestern regions of the country, the banana, mango, and jackfruit form the holy triad of fruits. Banana is associated with Devaguru Brihaspati, and it is a symbol of fertility and abundance. That's why a pair of banana trees with flowering branches is traditionally placed on either side of the entrance during weddings, religious festivals, and other special occasions. (*BBC Travel*, 2020) Interestingly, the banana plant is believed to be 'shudhdha' or pure since it does not grow from a seed that has been spat from someone's mouth. The plant must be planted and nurtured before it can produce fruit, and once harvested, it dies. Therefore, it plays a vital role in the initiation of the kola. The banana used is 'kadali'. After the bunch of bananas is cut, no important functions or ceremonies are held in the house or village where the kola is to take place. They cannot leave the village or spend nights outside the boundaries. Some food restrictions are also followed. The banana plant's stem is also used to prepare various objects in a kola ritual, like the geometric baskets where sacred items are kept. It is also used in the preparation of the *ani*. The banana stem is strong but it also allows to be penetrated owing to its fibrous composition. Thus, it can easily be installed on moulds.

Purification of the Land

Following the fixing of the date for the Kola ritual comes a very important step: the ceremonial cleansing of the site where the performance is to take place. An auspicious time, known as 'muhurtha' (or mahurat in Hindi) is set for this procedure as well, which includes tilling the soil, levelling the land, etc. Whether it be the sthaana or a location in the vicinity of the temple to which the deity is attached, or even within the confines of a household's yard, the purification process involves the use of a cow dung solution, a revered agent of purification in the region's ancient customs.

As the day of the Kola ritual draws near, preparations are made to adorn the dancing area with a variety of natural decorations, including mango leaf garlands, coconuts and tender leaves of coconut called 'siri'. The sacred area is further enhanced by the presence of a banana stem and other such offerings. The madiwala, a member of the washerman community, is tasked with spreading a ritually cleansed sheet of cloth on the designated spot where the deity's paraphernalia is later placed. The performance itself is conducted under a makeshift roof known as a 'dompe' or 'chappara'. This is similar to the Hindi word 'chappad' which roughly translates to an enclosure. As a symbol of good luck, it is customary to cut a bunch of bananas (kayila) and hang it in front of the performance area. This act is believed to bring good fortune and ensure the success of the sacred ritual.

A Recollection of the Pre-ritual Preparations at Shishila

After inhaling tonnes of dust on the ongoing highway construction enroute to Belthangady from Mangalore, I was finally welcomed by the greenery of dense palm farms that dotted the surroundings as soon as I crossed Uppinangady.

My destination was the famous Shishileshwara temple, located in a village called Shishila, about thirty kilometres from Dharmasthala, which housed a self-manifested 'linga'. The temple was nestled in the embrace of the Kapila river, sparkling serenely amidst hills that stood guard on all sides. Like all Indian temples, Shishileshwara had its share of legends. Locals believed that worshipping at this temple and feeding the fish in the Kapila river would cure one of all skin ailments. The river was, therefore, a restricted area for fishing, extending up to two kilometres around the temple.

But my actual destination was something else. I was there to witness a kola that night. So, after offering my prayers at the temple, I moved towards the area where the kola was scheduled to take place. Some of the main deities were Bermer, Shiraadi and Chakravarthy Kodamanithaya. As I had arrived early, I was able to witness the preparations that preceded the ritual dance. Thanks to my companion, Shashank Nellithaya, who was officiating the kola, I was able to interact with the performers and gain insight into their artistry.

The kola dancer's entire family was involved in the preparations, with three little children frolicking around while keenly observing their parents' skillful artistry. One of the kids was practicing by weaving a miniature basket made of banana stem. An elderly lady took charge of working on the 'siri,' the tender leaves of the coconut palm that are used to make the traditional skirt for the kola dancer. Her precise slicing of the leaves was a sight to behold. Once sliced, they are balled up and kept aside.

Others were engrossed in decorating the 'ani,' the headdress for the performer. Meanwhile, a relative, possibly an uncle, was meticulously carving out a *mugga* (mukha) or mask of Panjurli from an areca leaf sheath. The scene was bustling with activity and infused with a sense of anticipation for the upcoming kola.

Areca and Indian Ceremonies

For the uninitiated, areca is a very significant part of almost all auspicious ceremonies in India. Indeed, India is the world's largest producer of this cash crop, accounting for more than 50% of global production. Among the top producing states are Karnataka, Kerala and Assam. The areca palm is the source of the areca nut, which is traditionally consumed as supari with paan (betel). The word areca is itself derived from its original name along the southwestern coast—adekkya. The Tulu word is bajjayi.

The humble areca, often mistaken for a nut but, to clear the air—it is a fruit that hardens as it dries. Areca takes the phrase 'hardened by life' quite literally. Picture it poetically, and suddenly it's the coconut's pint-sized sibling without water or flesh. The areca palm boasts of leaves that are similar to those of a coconut palm but are smaller in size. Its lower portion, which encircles the stem, is known as a sheath. The leaf sheath of the areca palm is a hard biodegradable fibrous material, and it is estimated that India produces around 1,000 million areca nut leaf sheaths each year, weighing approximately 2.33 lakh tonnes. Dried-up areca leaf sheaths are utilized as firewood and also to manufacture disposable plates and fibre. During my father's childhood days, he recollects with nostalgia moments when he and his friends would sit on a sheath of areca, taking turns to be pulled from the top by the other kids, enacting a game of boat-ride during their vacations.

Since it is such an integral part of the coastal culture, you will see some product of the areca palm in the spirit worship of Tulu Nadu. Similarly, in naagamandala, which is a form of ritualistic serpent dance, the artist literally bathes in the tiny beads of areca nut flowers.

Bhandaara

In the lead up to the kola ritual, the bhandaara—the collection of sacred objects and paraphernalia—is of utmost importance. Typically, the bhandaara is housed in the sthaana or kone (room) throughout the year, but during the kola, it is transported to the place of the ritual. As mentioned before, this can be either a designated location or a makeshift structure in the kodiyadi. In my travels to kolas at Belmannu and Bandadi, I was privy to the delicate and precise process of transporting the bhandaara. Each object was picked up and carried in a particular order, evoking a sense of reverence and ritualistic importance. When the kola is happening at someone's home, then the bhandaara is carried from kone or sthaana by the family members who cover their foreheads and waists with a white drapery. The madhyasthar performs the act of madipu panpuna (madhu panpuna or paari panpunna)–the art of invoking the spirit with words, at different stages, and to speak on behalf of both the family and the daiva. My readers from the Tulu region would be familiar with this, but for non-Tuluva readers who might need a visual reference of procession, I recommend watching the music video of the adapted Tulu folk song, 'Va porluya' from *Kantara*.

In that music video you can notice how the bhandaara is carried in an ornate palanquin, adding a regal touch to the already sacred proceedings. The circumambulation of the sthaana and walk to the performance area is accompanied by the music of the 'vaadya' band. The route leading to the performance space is now illuminated with the aid of modern-day tube lights on either side. However, in the olden days, torches, or mashaals, provided the necessary illumination. Present-day observances frequently rely on bright LED lights, but certain locales remain steadfast in their adherence to time-honoured methods, where artificial lighting is strictly forbidden. In such instances, photography is also prohibited, as flashes of artificial light could potentially disrupt the sanctity of the proceedings. In those select precincts, the atmosphere truly appears hallowed, and attendees are transported to an otherworldly realm. Nonetheless, the current era's focus on taking photographs and creating reels of the performances has supplanted a more profound appreciation of these sacred performances. It is difficult to say whether it is right or wrong, because on one hand it spreads one's culture to the farthest corners of the world, while on the other, the viewer is losing out on capturing the priceless moments of a performance in their minds. So much dependence on hard disks and cloud storage!

When the bhandaara arrives at the designated place at the performance area, it is kept on a staired structure. The idol of the deity is kept at the centre. The other objects are also placed nearby along with offerings in the form of rice, tender coconut, flowers, etc.

Yenne Boolya

This step is of utmost importance and marks the beginning of the kola artist's preparations to perform the ritualistic dance. The representative of the organizer offers unhusked rice in a 'tadpe' or winnowing basket. Then he is offered ceremonial oil along with arecanut. The kola artist announces thrice that he is going to take the 'yenne-boolya'. An interesting observation is that many ritualistic actions throughout the kola ceremony are repeated thrice, such as sprinkling of water or dropping of milk. The repetition of actions three times might be attributed to Shaivite influence. This is followed by the granting of a plate of oil which the artist receives. He applies the oil on his skin, symbolic of purifying the human body to allow the spirit to enter, and then uses the same to mix colours for the make-up procedure.

In some kolas, the artist undergoes a transformative experience, which may include trembling and other noticeable manifestations. From my own firsthand observations, I've witnessed the artist passionately striking a steel plate against their head, resulting in visible deformation of the vessel. While these actions may evoke a sense of awe, it's important to note that they are part of the spiritual connection experienced by the artist. As the artist becomes a vessel for spiritual presence, I have often felt a profound sense of energy in the atmosphere, stirring deep emotions. Following this, the artist adorns themselves in attire symbolizing the specific spirit deity they will embody. The recitation of a sandi or part of the paaddana with the beats of a tembare (a type of drum) accompanies this transformation, aligning the artist with the spirit deity whose essence they channel.

The Fire Ritual

The priest who officiates the proceedings starts with a purification ritual by stacking up small logs of sticks on a plantain leaf. Then he kindles a fire. The smoke from this fire is believed to purify the environment. The water used in this process is used for sprinkling on objects to purify throughout the ritualistic dance. This form of havan, known as soma, is performed under a balluli. This symbolically represents the vayu tattva or wind aspect while the chappara or roof represents aakasha or sky, and charuva or bali represents the prithvi or earth. These three should be in a straight line. The balluli, thus, is a hanging object made from coconut and grains of pingaara at the centre, surrounded by strips of siri, and tied up by garlands of jasmine and abbalige (firecracker flower or Crossandra).

Important Flowers Used in the Ritual

Coastal Karnataka is a land that is abundant in natural resources, and among its treasures are some of the most exquisite flowers that this world has ever seen. These flowers, which are considered to be of great significance, play an integral role in the kola rituals and spirit worship of the region. In fact, the mere mention of these flowers transports me to a divine garden filled with mystical aroma.

At the forefront of these floral treasures is the majestic jasmine, or mallige as it is locally known. This flower is ubiquitous in the region and is used in various religious ceremonies and offerings to deities in temples. Its sweet fragrance and delicate beauty have made it a favourite among the devotees, and it is also given as prasada during kola rituals. Mallige is considered to be very dear to deities like Satyadevathe and Kallurti. If someone falls sick or has misplaced something but can't recollect where, then the person offers a garland of mallige to Satyadevathe or Kallurti, in return for speedy recovery of health or memory.

A flower that is unique to the coastal region of Karnataka and Kerala is the red lxora, or kepula as it is locally known. There is an interesting story behind the etymology of ixora. The flower derives its name from the Sanskrit word 'Ishvara', as the Portuguese who once had their presence in the region associated this flower with the Hindu God Shiva. This stunning flower is known for its medicinal properties, and is used to cure skin diseases according to Ayurvedic scriptures. It is used both in the rituals and the decorations of the ani and the performing artist during kola. The flower is particularly dear to Koragajja. Red ixora or kepula is so important to the region that Tulu Nadu's flag's dominant colour is inspired by it.

Another flower used is the crossandra, or kanakambra or abbalige, which is often used in garlands and temple offerings.

Its bright orange hue adds a touch of warmth and vibrancy to any setting, and it is believed to hold great significance in kola rituals and performances. It is used as a decoration on the ani and crown of the kola artist. The leaves of this flower is also used in some rituals.

The marigold, or chendu hoovu in the local language, is another flower that is widely used in the region. If you attend a kola then you will find garlands of yellow and orange hanging almost all around the performance area. Its bright orange and yellow hues are said to bring good luck and prosperity, and it is generally seen in many rituals and ceremonies across India.

Finally, there is the pingaara or areca flower, which may not seem like a flower at first glance, but technically is the bud of the areca palm's flowers. This small bright yellow bud, which grows during late spring or early summer, has male and female flowers on the same inflorescence. The whole bud is plucked and used for different veneration ceremonies of daivas and naagas in Tulu Nadu.

These flowers are just a glimpse into the rich cultural fabric of the coastal region of Karnataka, and their inclusion in the kola ritual signifies the nativity and antiquity of the spirit worship in Tulu Nadu.

The Transformation

The application of makeup in preparation for the kola is an elaborate and meticulous process. Reserved is a corner in the ritual area specifically designated for the purpose. It is in this space that the artist and his family undertake the intricate artistry necessary for the man to transform into the daiva. After purifying himself with oil, the artist begins the application of makeup. While most of the dyes used are derived from natural sources, I have heard that these days, some may be chemical in origin. Depending on the nature of the spirits, the primary base hues could be yellow, an array of beige tones, red, or black. As we journey southwards into Kerala, a striking dominance of red and its hues pervades the makeup, accompanied by the intricate designs characteristic of theyyam.

Positioned mightily in the make-up area is the formidable 'gaggara', while a lamp casts a warm glow from a nearby perch and a hand mirror is firmly placed before the artist. First, he wears a band on his head which keeps his hair from falling on his forehead. He picks up the base colour in his palm, puts drops of the ceremonial oil and mixes it. The initial step involves the application of the base colour onto the face, followed by a dusting of white powder. Thereafter, the intricate artwork which embellishes the artist's visage is carefully added. The eyebrows are drawn in bold strokes of black, while other features are brought to life with varying shades of white, red, and so on. These delicate nuances vary depending upon the spirit deity that the artist embodies. For instance, Panjurli may be (not at all times) distinguished by a third eye adorning the centre of the forehead, while Kallurti is marked by an intricate pattern of white dots on her face. Ferocious spirits such as Chamundi are enhanced by a tongue extension drawn beneath the lips, creating a frightful impression. The artistry of the face painting is a testament to the artist's inherent talent, cultivated through years of meticulous observation and practice.

Following the meticulous process, the kola artist proceeds to adorn himself with flower garlands and ornaments. In some spirit deities, a 'pingaara' is worn over each ear under the ornamental serpent-faced earpiece. This is followed up by the costume wearing. For the majority of these deities, the dancer dons a vibrant ensemble consisting of a predominantly red upper and lower garment, adorned with frills and embellishments throughout. What sets this costume apart is the iconic symbol of Tulu Nadu, prominently imprinted on the back. In the case of female deities, the artist drapes a saree, while for androgynous deities representing both male and female manifestations, the costume is tailored accordingly to depict the unique duality.

After wearing their costume, the artist wraps an areca leaf sheath on his feet that covers the area from the shin to the ankle like a pair of protective socks. He places a burning incense stick or two on top of his crown.

Gaggaradichi

The sacred ritual of gaggaradichi is a momentous occasion during the kola ceremony, where the kola artist adorns his feet with the auspicious anklets known as 'gaggara'. These ceremonial anklets are hollow and oval-shaped, filled with beads that produce a sonorous jingling sound as the artist moves.

The arrival of the kola dancer, dressed up for the first part of the ritualistic dance, is an awe-inspiring moment. The grand theatrical style of his body language and facial expressions immediately sets the stage for a surreal experience. The incense stick pinned on top of his crown emits fumes that create a misty aura, enveloping the entire arena. The hollow, oval-shaped ceremonial gaggara jingles while it is placed on a banana leaf. After an haarathi (aarti) of the deity, the dancer accepts flowers and throws the petals in the air all around. His rhythmic shaking increases as he collects the gaggara in his hands, fastens the rope attached to it around his palms, and waves it around in all directions before seeking permission to wear it from the important members of the village or house.

The initial dance is a sight to behold, with the music of the taase (a variant of taasha drum), dol (a variant of dhol) and naadaswaram (a wind instrument) in the background picking up tempo and the artist's movements becoming more vigorous. However, the true brilliance of the dance is lost when translated into mere words or sentences in a book.

Finally, the artist stops his circumambulations and rhythmic movements of the body, and his assistant helps him wear the gaggara. The other assistants come forward with water to drink and a towel to fan the artist, who, under all that costume and vigorous dancing, is understandably tired. And yet, this is just the beginning of the ritualistic dance.

The Holy Anklet

The intriguing connection between the gaggara and its counterpart, the chilambu anklet worn by revered oracles in Kerala, adds a fascinating layer to cultural parallels. Notably, a distinctive feature of the chilambu is the inclusion of an insignia representing the weapon associated with the deity. It's noteworthy that in Tamil culture, a variation of this anklet is referred to as silampu, further highlighting the nuanced variations in similar cultural elements across diverse regions. In the spirit dances of Africa, Bali and Tibet, as previously discussed in an earlier chapter, a striking similarity emerges—the presence of anklets gracing the dancers' movements. The resonance of this shared element underscores the universality of certain cultural expressions, transcending geographical boundaries and echoing the common threads that weave through diverse traditions. The significance of these anklets in ritualistic dance is immense, and they are believed to serve as a powerful conduit between the dancer and the spirit deities.

Adorning the Skirt

At the make-up area, one will come across an assemblage of 'siri' or coconut palm's tender fronds that are deftly bundled and neatly placed. These are meant to be draped as a skirt. The use of areca leaf sheath and coconut's fronds are proof of the dance form's antiquity.

One of the assistants will bring the siri skirt to the performance area. The dancer proceeds to unveil the verdant coils and commence draping them around the waist. The overhanging strands that graze the ground are promptly severed with a snip by the artist's assistant. The artist commences to perform a choreographed dance christened as sirinalike. Here, the kola dancer dips his fingers into the bristling web of the siri skirt, securely clasping it for a momentous span of time, before artistically letting it go. A prayer follows this ritual, as the artist's spirit gradually becomes possessed, akin to the waxing moon ascending the sky. He groans into the air as the possession happens.

The Moment of Possession

As the evening breeze blew and the cool night settled in, I journeyed through the narrow untarred roads to a small village near Bajpe, where I was to witness a family kola ritual. The captivating performance of Kallurti, followed by the 'nudi' session, left me in awe. After the artist had returned to his normal attire, I approached him with my friend and introduced myself as a writer, eager to learn more about his experience.

'At what stage did you get possessed? Were you aware of it?' I inquired.

'It's similar to how a television remote works,' the artist explained. 'When you press it, you don't see the transition, but you see that the channel has changed.'

The artist's simple yet brilliant response lingered with me long after that night. The possession, as he described it, is akin to kindling a fire with dry twigs or a matchstick—the spark remains for a brief moment, but it is enough to ignite the prepared log of wood. This brings to mind the insightful explanation of 'mooji mukkaal galige'. The deep trance coupled with music and drum-beatings infuse into the dancer, the spirit of divinity that is being propitiated (Updhyaya, 2002, pg no 34).

The emphasis, according to this, is given to the importance of music, faith of the spectators, and sincerity of the artist in facilitating possession. Much like how a wet log or a barren matchstick would fail to ignite a fire, an absence of any of these crucial elements, according to local beliefs, would hinder the occurrence of possession.

The Science Behind Possession

In the context of any possession ritual (not limiting to kola), the process of spirit possession may be seen as a manifestation of an altered state of consciousness or trance state. The term consciousness is of utmost importance here. This ethereal state is often induced through rhythmic movements, musical cadences, meditative practices, or hypnotic techniques, which are known to produce distinct alterations in perception, cognition, and behavior. Coming to the kola ritualistic dance, the kola artist engages in repetitive movements such as spinning, swaying, or shaking, which may induce a deep and immersive trance state. The amalgamation of the physical exertion, rhythmic movements and sensory stimulation may help to transform the medium's state of consciousness, allowing them to be possessed by the spirits that are believed to reside in the sacred realm of maya.

Psychologically, this transformation of consciousness may be interpreted as a form of dissociation or absorption. The artist becomes so entranced by the ritual and the sensations they are experiencing that they are momentarily dissociated from their self-awareness, becoming more receptive to suggestion. This may include self-suggestion which is a form of auto-hypnosis. The person will not be able to recall what had happened while he was possessed. Something that was discussed in the section on trance mediumship earlier.

The kola dance ritual's cultural and religious context plays a crucial role in shaping the medium's experience of spirit possession. Their unique beliefs and expectations about possession and the artist or medium's role can affect how they perceive the ritual and how others interpret their behavior. Spirit possession is significant in the field of hypnosis and psychology, as it bears a striking resemblance to conventional hypnotic phenomena, suggesting the presence of an underlying hypnotic mechanism. Overall, the intricate process of spirit possession in a kola dance ritual involves a multifaceted interplay of physical, psychological, cultural and spiritual factors, and no single explanation currently exists.

Kaarnika

Kaarnika means miracles or extraordinary feats. The dancer receives a burning torch, or 'jeetige', which varies in make according to the type of spirit. The torch could be composed of metal with a solitary flame, known as the koljeetige, or feature five flames, referred to as the panchajeetige, or perhaps a simple arrangement of tied-together dried coconut leaves, commonly known as the thootte. He then positions himself erect with a slight bend forward, bringing the burning torch close to his chest, and demonstrating his power. This stage of the performance involves exhibiting miraculous abilities that showcase the might of the spirit that has taken possession of the artist's body. The artist possessed by the daiva, leaves with the torch to give salutations to the village deity, the deities of all the directions.

The jeetige, or burning torch, is shown to the ganas and other minor spirits present in the spirit realm. This is followed by an offering of a tender coconut, or bonda, as a sign of honour to the deity. The purpose of this display is to inform the other spirits that the deity is present and being honoured by the people. Once this offering is made, the artist returns to the chappara and shows the jeetige to the four legs of the structure. Certainly, the detailed steps elucidate that the contemporary kola dance, with 'rasa' and 'bhaava', is a sophisticated and meticulously defined practice, closely aligned with the nuanced grammar of performance arts distinctive to the region.

After this, the artist, who is now possessed by the daiva, approaches the most important members of the community and shows them the jeetige. The objective of this ritual is to gaze upon the deity's visage through the fire. This may also be a mark of showing respect to the dignitaries. The dancer also honours the musicians and gives a garland of flower.

During certain moments of the ceremony, deities may demand that spectators get up and show respect. However, in most cases, people get up and join their hands in obeisance as the deity presses the jeetige against its chest. Throughout the time, a 'chaakiridaar' or assistant carries a vessel containing oil and keeps pouring it in the torch so that it isn't put off. But why is fire so important?

Fire—A Symbol of Power and Transformation

While attending a kola in Karkala, one young man sitting next to me jokingly suggested that the flame from the torch (jeetige) provided the spectators with the light they needed to perceive the deity's divine aura, as illumination was scarce in ancient times. From an evolutionary perspective, this may be correct. Fire holds great significance in numerous cultures and religions, where it has become an emblem of passion, energy, vitality, destruction, chaos and death. It can represent the divine spark or spirit within all living beings or seen as an embodiment of the divine itself. In the Vedic tradition, fire, or agni, is viewed as one of the five sacred elements or panchabhutas, forming the perceived material existence, where it exists at three levels—on earth as fire, in the atmosphere as lightning, and in the sky as the sun. As per beliefs, this triple presence accords Agni as the messenger between the deities and human beings. Even though the spirit worship of Tulu Nadu, according to erudite scholars, is believed to predate the Vedic scheme of things, fire as a symbol of power and transformation remains significant. Let me put it this way—the discovery of fire predates all forms of religion.

So, from an evolutionary perspective, fire was essential for human survival and development. According to English anthropologist, Richard Wrangham, the ability to cook food with fire made it easier to digest and provided more energy, which contributed to the development of larger brains and a competitive advantage over other animals. From a simpler point of view, fire provided warmth and light, which protected early humans from predators and enabled them to live in colder climates. Even to this day, people camping in the woods use fire to ward off wild animals. Additionally, fire was instrumental in tool-making and agriculture and other technologies' development.

Psychologically, fire has a primal and potent effect on the human psyche. Fire's unpredictable and dangerous nature triggers a survival response in the brain, while its captivating and mesmerizing qualities can induce a state of trance or meditation. People have used fire in spiritual and religious ceremonies for thousands of years as a symbol of purification, transformation, and rebirth. Fire's light and warmth can also foster a sense of community and social bonding, bringing people together around a fire to share stories, music and food. Thus, the evolutionary and psychological significance of fire has contributed to its continuing power and sacredness in human culture. Perhaps, this is the reason why fire is an integral part of most primitive religious customs of the world.

Adorning the Ani

The kola artist is assisted by his aides to embellish the ani, an exquisitely carved ornamental garb that is positioned behind the head, imbuing the bearer with a divine halo. The palm leaves, flowers, banana stem, silver ornaments and red cloth adorning the ani are crafted with great care and precision, resulting in a breathtaking masterpiece. The size and shape of the ani may vary, akin to the 'mudi' of theyyam, and some spirit deities may not even have an ani. Jakkelani, another ornamental costume is worn at the waist towards the front side of the artist. Once bedecked in his finery, the dancer assumes his seat and proceeds to narrate the paaddana, donning the mugga or the face mask of the spirit deity, which may be fashioned from materials such as areca leaf sheath, gold or silver, depending on the organizers' resources. Finally, the artist takes to the dance arena, resplendent in all his grandeur.

The next step is the offering of badikara, a sacred vessel in the shape of a kalash, fashioned from clay or silver, and filled with auspicious objects like rice, pingaara, betel-leaf, gandha (sandal paste), coconut and so on. The mukkaldi presents the badikara to the arena and moves around with it before the kola artist, who tries to acquire it but the mukkaldi dances away, swaying in a mesmerizing manner. After multiple circumambulations, the pot is ultimately surrendered to the artist. In certain kolas of rajandaivas, the divine dancer then rides in a bandi or cart, but these rituals may differ or be absent in other kolas.

After this, the dancer takes the bell and the weapon of the spirit like kadsala (type of sword) or beththa (type of wand). The chowrie fan is also given. The artist now dances in his full form and this vigorous dance can last for some time. He once again goes into that trance mode with the help of multiple circumambulations, crescendo of the music, fireworks exploding in the background, etc.

Disputes & Settlements

With a rhythmic shaking of the leg and the jingling of the gaggara, the artist sits upon a bench or chair, serving as a conduit between the mortal realm and the sacred. The words spoken by the artist possessed by daiva is called nudi, and this step is called nudi panpuna. Through the mediator or the madhyastar, the spirit speaks to the organizers, summoning them in a hierarchical order and demanding to know the reason for its invocation. It is then that the organizers offer their devotion and duty to the daiva, beseeching the spirit to accept the offerings of the faithful and forgive any transgressions. For the participants, the possessed dancer transcends inert idols and rocks, embodying the essence of the daiva. During this period, the spirit is believed to impart wisdom, resolving conflicts, and providing answers to the questions posed by the assembled devotees, believed to dispense a form of justice. I will elaborate on such sacred practices in greater depth in the next chapter.

Aavara

In the course of the kola, the deity is not just venerated through physical offerings but also through the presentation of food. The primary deity is typically bestowed with cooked rice, which is then arranged in a basket-like structure. In some cases, offerings may include poddollu (popped rice) and jaggery. For more ferocious spirits like Guliga, however, chicken may be required. I am reminded of a kola I witnessed at a brahmin's house in Bajpe where the offerings in front of Guliga consisted of popped rice, moode, tender coconut and, instead of a hen, a large ash gourd was placed. The reaction from Guliga was particularly comical as he began gesturing and inquiring from the mukkaldi if the hen had been hidden behind the kodiyadi. This caused quite a stir amongst the audience who could not contain their laughter. When the mukkaldi finally revealed that no non-vegetarian food was prepared or offered in the house, Guliga slammed his forehead in regret. In another kola in Bandadi, the Guliga wanted a cold drink to go with the diet.

Departure

As the night wears on, the kola ritual continues. After the food offerings have been made to the deities, it is time to bid them farewell. The mukkaldi brings a pot of water and dips a pingaara into it, sprinkling the water on the kola artist. The ritual symbolizes the departure of the spirit from the artist's body, returning to its ethereal realm. Just like in the beginning, there was 'yenne boolya', now the organizers offer 'piri boolya' to the kola artist. Piri means end and piripuna means departure in Tulu. The artist is also offered milk. So, in some parts of Tulu Nadu, this is synonymous with the completion of kola. If someone says, 'I'll offer milk to a daiva', then that means a kola must be organized for the daiva, at the end of which the dancer will be offered milk to drink.

The musicians lay down their instruments, and the devotees offer their offerings. They also receive their prasaada from the daiva. The atmosphere is filled with a sense of peace and reverence. As the night draws to a close, the first light of dawn begins to appear on the horizon. The kola artist gradually returns to his normal state, free from the possession of the spirit. The long night of the kola ritual thus comes to an end, and the villagers can now rest, content in the knowledge that they have paid their respects to the deities and honoured their traditions. Many kolas happen from sunset to sunrise, while some also happen during the daytime.

Conclusion

These are the steps involved in a kola ritual. As previously mentioned, this description is quite generalised, and the actual practice can vary significantly from place to place and from daiva to daiva. To gain a deeper understanding of these steps, I personally attended multiple kola performances over an extended period of time. Sometimes, only one spirit deity is invoked at a time. Only after the dance is finished does the next one get ready. Occasionally, two dancers perform simultaneously, with one of them embodying a banta or mute spirit deity. In some instances, three or more may perform together. For instance, I visited a kola in Kudupu where Kallurti, Chamundi, and Kalkuda performed together. In another kola, I witnessed Panjurli and Guliga sharing the arena. Sometimes, the invoked spirit deity is offered a variety of delicacies other than the usual offerings. The variations in performance styles, the interplay between multiple deities, and the unique offerings presented all contribute to the diversity and captivating nature of this tradition.

9

Nudi Panpunna — The Justice of the Spirit Deities

AS THE KOLA RITUAL HITS A CRESCENDO, A CRUCIAL moment in the event known as nudi panpuna takes place. At this stage, the divine dancer serves as a vessel for the spirit deity, conveying sacred words known as nudi. These words, believed to originate from the daiva, carry immense significance to the devout followers of the ritual. The nudi is regarded as a gateway to divine blessings and serve as a source of hope for those seeking solutions to their problems that couldn't be solved through materialistic means. Through the kola dancer, the daiva provides assurances of remedies that according to believers, bring about relief, imbuing the ritual with a sense of sacredness and healing. While it can be debated whether these words are spoken by a human or the divine, the value it provides to the believers cannot be denied. The kola ritual, with its profound focus on community, serves as a beacon of hope, bringing individuals together in a spirit of harmony and well-being. Let me take you through some of the incidents that I had witnessed or heard from others during my research on the subject.

Incident 1: The Forgotten Vow

During a kola ritual in their village, a family from a metropolitan city sought guidance regarding constant hindrances in the sale of ancestral property and consulted a kola dancer portraying the daiva.

They stood before the kola dancer seated on a red chair at the center of the arena, his rhythmic leg movements suggestive of spiritual possession.

Communicating cryptically in archaic Tulu, the dancer initially spoke in riddles with references to maternal love, highlighting the importance of ancestral reverence. Further inquiry by the mediator revealed the neglect of the family's moola naaga and the presence of a serpent grove in the ancestral land.

As the consultation progressed, it became evident that family discord played a significant role, with the family's headman acknowledging strained relations with a female family member excluded from property discussions.

The dancer, speaking as Kallurti, likened this discord to harming a maternal figure, warning of negative consequences. Ultimately, a solution was proposed during the nudi session: prioritize familial reconciliation, including the neglected female family member, before seeking divine intervention at her shrine. The visibly humbled headman expressed gratitude for the guidance received.

Poorva Kattle and Daiva's Justice

In the long gone past, the veneration of the spirits served not only as an expression of spiritual devotion but also played a crucial role in the 'poorva kattle' or the ancient administrative system of the region. During those times, the region was divided among several dynasties. The smallest unit of this system was the family. An 'ooru' denotes dispersed homesteads of families and tenants, toiling over rice or areca nut cultivation, nestled around the central 'manor' of the chief. The 'ooru' formed a part, while 'maagane' comprised of a group of 'oorus', which in turn comprised a segment of a regional border or 'seeme' or 'naadu'. A faraway land that is outside the 'ooru' is 'paravuru'. The leader of the seeme was known as the arasu, ballal, odeya, etc. Arasu roughly translates to king, and the 'gadipattinaru', or holder of the throne, while the manors under his purview were the property of diverse 'guttu', or junior lineages. At the head of each guttu stood the 'guttinaaru'. The 'guttumanes' are akin in prestige to the manor houses of the British, while being a structural cousin of the traditional 'Nalukettu' architectural style of Kerala. Each spirit has a jurisdiction, based on which it could be known as 'ooruda daiva', 'graama daiva', 'seeme daiva', 'illada daiva', etc. Each daiva wielded influence over a distinct domain, demarcated by geographical boundaries. Thus, the daiva governing the smallest unit fell under the jurisdiction of higher-ranking deities.

Individuals who held faith in the daiva were extremely cautious not to incur their displeasure. In ancient times, when settlements were sparse and villages were often enveloped by dense forests, the intimidating and ominous presence of spirits was perceived as a manifestation of the untamed aspects of nature.

Although the concept of Bhutas instills fear, but in accordance with folk beliefs, it is suggested that righteous souls have no cause for fear. This concept illustrates the idea of 'daiva's justice', which is perceived as a form of divine justice that becomes evident to mortals when the daiva, communicating through a kola dancer or a darshana patri, speaks at the conclusion of the kola ceremony.

Omens

Omens play a significant role in various religious practices across the world, often interpreted as signs from the spirit realm. It's common to observe artists or officiants using areca flowers or betel leaves to seek answers. For instance, they might pluck strands from a pingaara (areca flower), toss them in the air and catch it for count, or toss a betel leaf to discern which side it falls on. In recounting the incident that I introduced in the beginning of this chapter, it becomes apparent how the daiva communicates with families through the intermediary. The family from the metropolitan city that had sought out the kola dancer was in no way affiliated with the land, and the daiva possessing the artist should ideally have no knowledge about their background. It is worth noting that most elders in coastal Karnataka and Kerala attempt to link any misfortune in the lives of city dwellers with the neglect of their moola naaga. If you recall, my quest for 'truth' began in a similar manner, leading me to an elder in my family who interpreted it in her own way and suggested something else. I was inquisitive and curious, so I kept on inquiring from people to people. This ultimately inspired me to set off on a journey to seek out my ancestor's naaga and daiva.

That being said, what I am suggesting here is that for city-dwellers who have settled far from their hometowns, it is highly likely that they are unable to attend their village's annual festivals or pay respects to their moola naaga or daiva on a regular basis. Many people who migrate to cities become ensnared in their urban tentacles and may never return to their villages. Their children may never learn of their ancestral roots. Many individuals from villages have migrated in search of improved living standards. As a result, migrants come into contact with people from different cultures and attempt to adjust their lifestyles to conform to urban norms. Unfortunately, this often results in neglecting their village traditions like kuladevata, naaga or daiva. Years later, sometimes generations later, when they face difficult situations in life that seem unsolvable, they get stuck. Consequently, when such a city dweller consults an oracle or an elder in the family with that problem, one of the first questions they are asked is, 'Have you recently paid tribute to your daiva or moola naaga?'

Incident 2: The Consoling Oracle

As the region was getting ready for the new year in April, I was attending a grand kola in Kudupu. This one had around a few thousand people in attendance and was happening in a huge ground. Once again, this was a Kallurti kola, and the darshana patri was possessed by Kallurti. Note that the darshana patri is not the same as a kola dancer. Here, the person acts like an oracle without adorning any facial makeup or costumes. A family from a faraway city, consisting of a father, twenty-something-year-old daughter and a thirty-year-old son, came forward with their problem.

The father informed the darshana patri that his daughter was not able to clear any exams. She was good in studies, yet when it came to examinations, she would never clear them. It had been like that for almost six to seven years because of which she has not been getting employment.

'How often do you visit your kuladevata?' The oracle asked.

'Once a year, and sometimes when I come here, I make sure that I visit the family deity,' the girl's father replied with joined palms and bowed head.

'Good, and that is why she has been keeping well all these years that you mentioned.'

The father nodded. The oracle picked up a few strands of pingaara, threw them into a winnowing basket. The mediator counted the strands, nodded his head after noticing the positive omen.

The oracle confidently went ahead to tell the mediator, 'Her problems will be solved. I think she is trying to get a job in the state administration (probably a government job), which she will when you do as I say, and then you will come back and offer a glass of milk.'

As mentioned before, the expression 'offering a glass of milk' means offering a kola to the daiva upon fulfillment of the wish. Thus, the consoling words of the oracle calmed the family that had been struggling with anxiety over the future of their daughter's career.

Style of Speech

Throughout the kola ritual, the dancer portrays facial expressions and hand gestures which are quite symbolic and artistic in nature. An artist is thus an apt word for the dancer. Though not exactly similar, but these kinds of actions can be noticed in dance forms like Bharathanatyam, Kathakali, etc. The kola artists learn it purely by observation.

The way the possessed dancer speaks to the organizers and the audience is also quite unique. The language used differs from the everyday Tulu used by the people, and the artist uses a lot of idioms and phrases that are delivered in different modulations of voice.

This reminds me of a nudi session where the deity through the kola dancer was asked to settle a family problem. The dancer said, 'A mother's love is equal,' his voice lilted like a song. 'If you prick one eye of a mother, then the other eye will also shed tears. The two eyes represent you and your sibling, who are both equal for the old mother whom you have conveniently forgotten,' the dancer had paused for effect. Tension rose in the family. Then the artist broke the silence and explained, 'When one eye stabs the other, tears will drain from both eyes. When you treat your sibling unfairly then you will also be affected by grief and losses.'

Even while offering solutions to the problems asked by devotees, the artist changes his tone to suit the ruling that he is imparting.

What I noticed in both the incidents that I have recounted in this chapter till now is the difference in the tone used by the possessed artist. In the first incident, the artist used a commanding tone which sparked rage at the attitude of the city-dwellers. While in the second incident, the tone was consoling at best as the devotees that came forward with their problem were submissive and obedient. Come to think of it, this is how a wise teacher or a school's principal would behave. She will be strict and harsh with students who break the rules, while soft and uplifting towards those who follow them. The way this authority figure behaves impacts the psyche of the students.

Psychological Impact

The impact of a solution provided by a spirit medium (in general) on a troubled person's psyche cannot be underestimated. Often, those who seek guidance from a spirit medium are burdened with feelings of anxiety, uncertainty and helplessness. Yet, when the medium offers a solution, it serves as a beacon of hope and a source of control that can alleviate these negative emotions.

Moreover, the power of belief in the spirit medium and the efficacy of their solution cannot be understated. It provides comfort and reassurance, and the community may also rally behind those facing similar problems, offering solace and support. In some instances, the solution may entail a ritual or an action, which can be transformative, providing closure or resolution that can serve as a cathartic experience.

The overall psychological impact of the solution presented by a spirit medium can be affirmative and optimistic, offering a sense of hope, control, comfort, community and closure. However, it's essential to recognize that the effectiveness of the solution may vary based on the individual's beliefs and cultural background.

Incident 3: The Tree

During a kola, a community leader consulted the darshanapatri oracle and addressed a pressing issue dividing the village - the construction of a new private road within the temple's private premises that threatened an old peepal (ashwatha) tree.

The oracle, emphasizing its role as a protector of all villagers, declared its attachment to the tree and its unwillingness to see it completely removed. However, acknowledging the need for paved path for easier movement, the oracle offered a compromise. He suggested a solution that balanced progress with environmental and cultural concerns.

The villagers were advised to trim the branches obstructing the road path, allowing construction to proceed while preserving the core of the sacred tree. This decision resonated with the community's cultural reverence for the peepal tree and its ecological significance.

This approach highlights the potential for traditional practices to contribute to finding solutions that respect both cultural beliefs and practical needs.

10

Seeking the Satyas

WHEN I STARTED MY JOURNEY, I HAD LITTLE HOPE of finding my ancestor's serpent grove or successfully documenting the ancient practice of daiva aaradhane. Speaking of the research for this book, despite trying to connect with experts, initially I struggled to find the right people. Additionally, I was grappling with emotional and physical pain that almost made it impossible to proceed. I had stuttered, and the thought of giving up and returning to my cocoon crossed my mind. However, my spouse encouraged and suggested me to proceed after offering a prayer to Varte and Sathyadevathe at her ancestral home where I was staying at the time. Then I continued my journey through the mystical land of Tulu Nadu. I carried with me a seed of doubt, uncertain of what lay ahead. This journey was marked by numerous coincidences that I don't shy away from calling divine interventions. Like the arrival of Kariye and his men outside the door while we were discussing Kordabbu and Thannimaaniga. Yes, it was coincidence, but could the timing have been any better?

It wasn't just me; even those who became part of my journey were influenced by some kind of divine intervention that led them to agree to meet me. It so happened that on the midnight of 27 March, a madhyasthar, found himself serving as a mediator at a kola in a village south of Mangalore. During the nudi ceremony, the dancer who was possessed by the daiva, seized the mediator's right arm and spoke these words: 'Madhyasthare ... *the time has arrived*. You are well-known here and have been serving us faithfully. You haven't stepped on the delicate stem of a drumstick, nor have you held on to the fragile branches of a mango tree. *The time has arrived*. By embracing the daiva, you have stepped on the firm branches of a jackfruit, and holding on to the sacred branch of a sandalwood. *The time has arrived*. Your name shall transcend beyond the borders of the region when people from far will come looking for you. Just be ready ... this is the truth...'

Some thirty-two miles away, I was documenting information on daivaradhane from a young prodigy in Kudupu. Following a lengthy meeting, I found myself having to stay overnight in a hotel in Mangalore. I was trying to get in touch with a popular television personality and another renowned elder mediator of kolas. However, neither of them responded. Later, I met a friend of my father-in-law. When I revealed that I was documenting a non-fiction book on daiva aradhane and was seeking to connect with experts on the subject, he promised to do what he could.

It was at midnight that my phone lit up with a WhatsApp notification. Upon opening it, I found the contact details for a kola mediator staring back at me. Two days later, I met the mediator. He mentioned the words spoken by the daiva, coinciding with my arrival from Maharashtra. Again, was it a mere coincidence on this speck of dust in space called Earth, or was it propelled by mysterious forces beyond our perception?

In the depths of this land of spirit deities, where the daivas still dance on the edges of consciousness, I witnessed a truth that resonated with every fiber of my being. The practice of venerating these primordial deities, often seen as remnants of an earlier era, has not only endured the passage of time but has also evolved, fostering a strong connection between the people of this region and the daivas. For the believers of daivaaradhane of Tulu Nadu, daivas and bhutas are known as satya or the truth (*pl.* satyolu). While the practice of worshipping spirits or primitive deities may have vanished or merged into a larger organized religion in almost all parts of the world, the prevalence of spirit deities in the region proves how much the daivas mean to the people. The spirit of Tulu Nadu whispered its secrets to me, revealing the profound depths of belief that permeated the very air I breathed. The very air that my ancestors had breathed a century ago.

In the face of doubt and skepticism that often plague our modern world, the prevalence of spirit deities in coastal Karnataka stands as a testament to the enduring power of faith. Whether it is the daiva of Tulu Nadu, theyyam of Kerala or mhasobha of Maharashtra, the veneration of spirit deities is a reminder that even as the currents of change reshape the landscapes of spirituality and religion, certain truths refuse to fade into oblivion. They persist, etched upon the souls of the faithful, interwoven with the mosaic of their existence.

Through the course of my journey, I discovered that the satya, far from being mere myths or superstitions, were a lifeline for those who sought solace, guidance, and strength. Their presence resonated in every aspect of life, from the humblest sthaana to the grandest kolas. The daivas offered refuge to the weary, wisdom to the seeker, and a spiritual connection to something greater than ourselves.

In the crucible of my experiences, I shed the shackles of doubt and embraced the profound truth that dwelled within the hearts of the people of Tulu Nadu. As I allowed it to sway and dance away, the strings of caste, religion and language dissolved into the essence of truth that was above and beyond everything. For, in the dance of existence where the ethereal and the earthly entangle, it is the power of belief that propels us forward, that nurtures our souls, and that connects us to the infinite. And in that belief, in the eternal sacred realm, the spirit deities shall forever find their dwelling place, their presence felt by those who embrace the extraordinary, or in the language of the western mind—'embrace the light'.

Thus, as I bid farewell to the Satyolu of Tulu Nadu, I carry within me the indomitable enduring legacy of the daivas, the stories of oppression and revolt, and the unwavering truth that faith, in all its forms, has the power to transcend the limitations of our existence and illuminate the path to our deepest, most profound selves. However, I promise you, my reader, that this is just the beginning. I will continue my search for the truth in another land ... in another form of worship ... in another book.

The way this book started and proceeded on its own, like a giant wave carrying me forth, has been nothing short of a miracle. The cocoon that enshrouded me following the preceding year's tragedy dissolved. Along with it, the physical afflictions that had curtailed my ability to embark on long journeys faded. Those few months in Tulu Nadu not only led me closer to the discovery of my ancestral serpent grove, a mere stone's throw from Kateel, but I also lived a thousand lives that inspired me to finish this project. These thousand lives were not just mine; they belonged to every individual I encountered, every individual from those marginalized communities who kept this tradition alive, battling the tyrants of their time, and to the spirit deities whose stories of righteousness and revolt resonated within me. As articulated in the first chapter of this book, it was a voice that called to me, but I didn't know what it was then. Now, I know that the voice that called me was the voice of truth ... of satyolu ...

K. Hari Kumar
9 February 2024

PART 2
The Stories of Satyolu

A Note on Folktales

A FOLKTALE IS A SPECIFIC TYPE OF STORY WITHIN the broader context of folklore. Folklore is the cultural heritage of a community that includes a wide range of expressive forms, while folktale specifically refers to the narrative or story aspect of this cultural heritage. All of us have grown up listening to folktales mostly from our grandparents or an elderly relative. While growing up in Delhi, the arrival of May and June heralded a cherished period as schools shuttered their doors for the summer vacations. We would pack our bags and go on a trip to my native. For me, it was all about meeting my ajjis (maternal and paternal grandmothers). They lived in different cities and both would tell me folktales from their original native places (you see, one was born in Paanavally, Kerala and the other in Udupi, Karnataka, so I got the best of both worlds). These narratives unfolded realms inhabited by ghosts, goblins, heroes, gods and a myriad of fantastical beings. The enchanting tales acted as a palette, splashing the canvas of my imagination with vibrant hues from my formative years. Sometimes they told the same story but they had some subtle differences. And then I would argue with them, 'No, this is not what the other one told me.' Back then, I didn't understand that variability in oral literature was a real thing. Now I do.

Much like folktales from any region, the stories of daivas and heroes in Tulu Nadu boast multiple versions, adorned with subtle and not-so-subtle distinctions. Sometimes, the daivas are known by different names in different regions, adding to the complexity. It's plausible that the origin stories have been veiled by the sands of time, a sentiment echoed by many scholars. Folk deities emerge from local beliefs, and evolve through the syncretism of different cultural and religious influences, resulting in the emergence of new deities or the reinterpretation of existing ones, thus, giving us new variations of the folktale. This is a global phenomenon.

The primary reason why folktales change so much is because they were not written down in the past. They were passed on from generation to generation orally. As they were recited verbally, from region to region, by people who adhered or were influenced by different pantheons of beliefs, a change in one word or ideology could result in an entirely different story as it trickled down multiple generations. This variability in oral traditions is a challenge. The oral transmission of folktales and poems was often influenced by the storyteller's memory, imagination, interpretation and even the audience's reactions. Over time, these stories would naturally evolve and be adapted to fit the cultural, social and political contexts of the communities in which they were being told. Additionally, as these stories were transmitted across different dialects, they would be further shaped and reshaped by new influences and contexts.

One contributing factor to the variability observed in narratives surrounding spirit deities is the belief that these entities possess the ability to translocate by attaching themselves to individuals or objects. For instance, a spirit may accompany a newly married woman to her husband's residence, situated in a different geographic region. In this new locale, the spirit may demonstrate miraculous occurrences, known as 'kaarnika,' and consequently receive veneration. However, the narratives surrounding this spirit in the new region are likely to diverge from those originating in its original place of association. Indeed, distinct stories of miraculous events attributed to the same spirit deity may emerge in each respective region. Over time, these narratives tend to evolve independently, resulting in significant divergence from the original accounts, with only fundamental aspects of the original spirit deity's nature being retained.

As a result, there is often no single definitive version of a folktale or poem, and it is not uncommon for different regions, cultures or even individuals to have their own unique variations of the same story. The beauty is in accepting that multiple versions of the same tale exist, and finding common ground that would unite everyone.

So, in the upcoming chapters, I've diligently endeavored to delve into a multitude of sources, weaving together my renditions of the folktales that have been an integral part of our upbringing. I have tried to expound upon the contextual intricacies to the best of my knowledge, providing readers unfamiliar with the culture of Tulu Nadu with a comprehensive understanding of the events unfolding in these narratives. The folktales presented in the forthcoming pages, although originating from a different era, may mirror the harsh realities of that bygone time. Transportation primarily relied on foot, and communication occurred through scrolls delivered by messengers. Punishments were often severe. These stories are from a time much before modern inventions, and are full of fantastical elements. While I have made efforts to soften their impact for modern readers, it is worth noting that they may contain elements that could unsettle contemporary sensibilities.

May my words serve as vessels, carrying forth the timeless tales of the daivas and heroes of Tulu Nadu, ensuring their enduring legacy and kindling a spark of curiosity within you to explore their depths further in times yet to unfold.

1
Satyamma Kallurti and Beera Kalkuda

IN TULU NADU, TWO REVERED SPIRIT DEITIES HOLD sway over the collective consciousness of its people. Kallurti and Kalkuda, their names whispered with utmost reverence, transcend the boundaries of ordinary spirituality. For, unlike other spirit deities whose origins lie within the realms of Kailasa or Vaikuntha, these ethereal spirit deities emerge from the very soil of this sacred region. Kallurti may also be known as Satyamma, Satyappe, Satyado Appe, Kallamma, etc. Kalkuda is also known as Biru, Veera or Beera Kalkuda.

Chapter 1 — Shambhu's Departure

Once upon a time, in the quaint village of Kellatta Marnadu lived Airavati (Eeravadi) and Shambu Kalkuda. Shambu was a renowned sculptor, known for his exquisite creations that captured the hearts of all who beheld them. The couple was blessed with four sons, each of whom went on to master a different craft—Yellana became a carpenter, Mallanna a blacksmith, Beeru a goldsmith, and Bikkuru worked with copper. He wanted his fifth child to be a sculptor.

One day, while Airavati was pregnant with twins, Shambu received countless summons via messengers from Belur and Belagola, requesting him to come and work on a sculpture of Gomateswara. Although he was hesitant to leave his pregnant wife behind, he eventually decided to go as the messages were sent long before, and he felt duty-bound. Shambhu supplied his pregnant wife with mustard, pepper, some dried coconuts, a pot of oil and a metal vessel. Thus, after making sure she had everything she needed to sustain herself for the duration of his absence, he prepared rice, starch water and other food for his journey. He sharpened his tools before embarking on his journey to Belagola.

As Shambu left his wife behind, his mind was clouded with confusion and uncertainty about whether he had made the right decision. However, he soon witnessed a few good omens on his path—a stream, a long hill, a tree to which an elephant was tied, and a banyan tree to which a horse was tied. These positive omens gave him hope and he continued on his journey undeterred. He passed through Santandadka, Kokkada, and Nirenki before finally reaching Belagola, ascending twelve steps of stone to enter the grand city.

As he made his way through the city, Shambu crossed three large yards, a painted chavadi, and a pillar of precious stones before finally arriving at the large courtyard where he awaited the king. The king arrived in grand fashion, sitting on a throne decorated with peacock feathers.

'Hail, Sire!' Shambu greeted the king with respect.

'Come, take a seat,' said the King.

'Why did you call for me, Sire?' asked Shambu Kalkuda.

Looking at the twilight sky after the sun had set, the king said, 'Now is not the time to discuss work. Take five sers (a unit of measurement) of rice and retire to your lodging for the night. Tomorrow, we shall speak about the work, and then you shall immediately start working.'

And so, Shambu retired to his lodging, grateful for the kindness of the king. As he lay down to rest, he wondered what kind of sculpture he would be creating and how he would do it justice. He hoped that he would be able to impress the king and make his family proud. The next day, he eagerly awaited his meeting with the king, ready to embark on his next great adventure.

The next morning, at sunrise, the king summoned Shambu Kalkuda and instructed him, 'I have heard of your talents and therefore, I want to give you a great responsibility.'

Kalkuda humbly bowed and waited for the king to explain his duties.

'I want you to make a grand basadi of a thousand pillars, seven gundas with its idols and grand gopuram outside. Above all, I want you to construct a grand, larger-than-life idol of Gomata,' The king instructed further, 'Construct in such a way that where the unlocking of one door sets in motion a harmonious opening of a thousand doors on their own, and closing one results in the closure of all. There should be a chamber for dancers, for lodging and structures for containing a lone elephant, horses and lions.'

'It will be done, sire. However, I wish to choose my own stones,' Shambu replied after hearing the king's demands.

'You can go to the quarry and take any stones you want,' the king said.

Shambhu proceeded to the quarry and prayed to the gods of all four directions. He found a cleft in the rock, and with his great power, he cut them into two. Thus, he began his work.

Chapter 2—Biru Wants to Know About His Father

A few years passed.

One day, while the king was taking a stroll to admire the grandeur of Shambu's work, the sculptor appeared before him and made a request.

'Your Majesty,' Shambu said, 'it has been many moons since I left my home. My wife was pregnant at the time, and I wish to visit her. I wish to see my children. Hold them in my arms if they are not grown up already. Would you be kind enough to grant me leave?'

The king, who had come to admire the sculptor's talent, readily granted him leave and presented him with gifts as a token of appreciation. As Shambu left for his home, the king continued to admire the sculptures that had made him famous in all the lands.

Meanwhile, at his home, Shambu's wife Airavati had given birth to twin children—Biru (Beera) and Kallamma (Satyamma). However, the children had never seen their father as he had been absent for so long. All the other children in the village refused to play with Biru, calling him a fatherless child.

The young Biru could bear it no longer and confronted his mother with a heavy heart. 'Mother, do I have a father?' he asked.

'Why do you ask such a question?' she inquired.

'The other children have been teasing me for a long time. They call me fatherless, and I have excused them once and then the second time. So, I have come to ask, my mother, tell me the truth as it is ... whether I have a father or not ... if you digress from the truth, then I will slice your throat,' the short-tempered boy said.

Airavati gasped in horror at the boy's words. 'Ayyo! You have a father.'

'Then where is he?'

'My dear son, when you were in my womb, he had to leave for work at Belagola. But I think it is high time he returned.'

'How do I know that you are telling me the truth?'

'Come with me!'

The mother went inside one of the rooms and the son followed. The room was filled with the sculptures and other achievements of his father.

'Look, these are all your father's works.'

The son looked around. His eyes gleamed with pride. His heart filled with joy. He had made up his mind.

'I can't wait for him to come back. I want to see him. I wish to see his works for which he was summoned,' Biru said with determination.

'But you are just a boy.'

'I may be a boy, but I wish to see my father. So, if your heart is true, and my father hasn't forgotten me, then I will meet him on the way,' said a determined young Biru Kalkuda.

Chapter 3 — A Fateful Encounter

Filled with the longing to see his father, Biru set out for Belagola, the city where Shambu had been working for so long. He soon passed the path that his father had traversed. After travelling much in the scorching heat, he came across a cool platform under a large tree, where he saw a horse tied up, and a man was resting. Biru went to the platform and sat on it, next to the man. As fate would have it, this man was none other than Shambhu Kalkuda. Biru did not realize that the man was his father, nor did Shambu know that the boy who had arrived was his son.

'Who are you, O young one? Where do you come from? Where are you going all alone?' Shambhu inquired.

Biru, feeling annoyed at the questions, replied, 'Why do you want to know all this? Do you pose these questions to all those you encounter on your path?'

The man responded calmly, 'No, child. I just inquired to know the truth.'

'Truth?' Biru calmed down and said, 'I come from the village Kellatta Marnadu. I am going to Belur.'

'Belur? Why are you going to Belur?'

'In search of my father,' Biru revealed with a tint of sadness.

'But why? Is he not with you?'

'When I was in my mother's womb, he left for work.'

Now, Shambu was getting suspicious. He asked, 'What's your father's name?'

'Shambu Kalkuda,' Biru revealed.

Shambu's eyes glowed with joy. He realized that the boy was his son, hugged him and kissed his cheek. Once again, the little boy got enraged and pushed his father away.

'Do you hug and kiss all the people you meet on the road?'

'Oh, dear child, I am so happy to see you.'

'But why?'

'You are my son, and I am the father you came looking for … Shambu Kalkuda.'

Biru was still skeptical and demanded proof. 'Tell me, if you are my father, what is my mother's name?'

'Airavati,' Shambu replied with a smile.

Biru's happiness knew no bounds. He immediately hugged his father. Both shared a moment of bonding.

'I am so thrilled, my son. When I left home, you were not even born, and now you have grown so much that you came searching for me. It is true that I am your father, and you are my son. Come, let's go home.'

But Biru refused to go home just yet. 'No, I won't go home now,' he insisted, his tone changing. 'I want to go to Belagola.'

'Why?'

'I want to see your work ... the fruits of your labour ... your creations.'

The father agreed, and together they journeyed back to Belagola.

As Biru and his father reached the city, Shambu proudly showed him his grand work, illuminated by the light of five torches. The sheer scale and beauty of the creations impressed the young boy greatly. However, as he looked closer, he noticed something amiss and pointed it out to his father.

'Everything looks great except for one thing,' Biru told his father.

'Why? Did you find a mistake?' Shambu asked with concern.

'Yes!' Biru exclaimed.

Shambu's face fell. 'Then you must show me, for I had made a vow that if I make one mistake then I shall amputate my arm and quit this profession.'

Biru then pointed out the mistake in one part of his father's creation. As Shambu examined it, he exclaimed, 'Rama, Rama! So many, including the king, have examined my work but none could find this mistake, but you, who was only born recently, was able to pinpoint this.'

Shambu grew anxious. 'If the King sees this mistake, he will give me the worst of punishments, for he has bestowed everything I needed for these creations. I would cut off my hands, but then what would be the use of this life? So, I am going to kill myself,' he said, picking up a knife from his girdle and slitting his throat.

As Biru watched his dying father, he declared, 'I am not going to let you down or dishonour your name. I am going to pick up your tools and finish your work. Before you breathe your last, teach me everything you know about your art.'

Thus, with his dying breaths, Shambu imparted his knowledge of stone masonry and sculpting to young Biru Kalkuda, who carried on his father's legacy with the same passion and dedication. He accomplished all that was set before him, surpassing even his father's deeds. His renown and repute crossed the borders of his realm, reaching far-flung kingdoms and beyond.

Chapter 4 — Bhairavarasu

In Karkala, there was a ruler by the name of Bhairavarasu. When he heard of Kalkuda's greatness, he summoned the young prodigy to his kingdom.

'I have heard so much about you, so I want you to make me the greatest statue of Gomata on this land,' Bhairavarasu revealed his wish.

'Your wish is my command,' said Biru and he began his work.

Years passed by before the grand statue was finally completed. The king summoned a multitude of five thousand people to raise the statue, but to no avail. It was then that Bhairavarasu spoke up, 'Oh Kalkuda, if you manage to raise the idol, I shall reward you with even greater gifts than before.'

As the sun began to set on the horizon, Biru Kalkuda placed his left hand under the statue and lifted it with the greatest of ease. The statue of Gomata was finally erected on its base. After completing his task, he turned to the king and requested his payment and bonus, 'Your Highness, it has been twelve long years since I left my home and came here. Please fulfill your promise and provide me with my rightful reward.'

But the king replied, 'Dear Kalkuda, it is now time for us to break our fast. Return at dawn tomorrow, and I shall present you with a befitting reward for your valiant efforts.'

The very next morning, Kalkuda arrived at Bhairavarasu's court, his heart full of hope and anticipation to return home after a long absence and reunite with his beloved mother and sister, Kallamma.

But Bhairavarasu had other plans. 'Kalkuda, you may keep all the gifts I have promised you, but I cannot allow you to create another idol that surpasses the magnificence of my Gomata in another land.'

'What do you mean, Sire?'

'I must take something from you to ensure that you do not continue such work elsewhere.'

'I do not understand. What are you going to take from me that shall stop me from creating another masterpiece out of stone?'

And then, Bhairavarasu rose from his throne with his sword and ruthlessly severed Kalkuda's left hand and right leg.

Kalkuda crumpled to the ground, but his spirit remained unbroken. With clenched teeth and eyes blazing with fury, he declared, 'I shall not be a useless wretch, and I vow never to even taste a single drop of water from the land of Karkala.'

And so, Kalkuda left Karkala and made his way to the kingdom of Venur, determined to forge a new path for himself, despite the challenges he now faced.

Timmanna Ajila, the ruler of this new kingdom, greeted Kalkuda with open arms, pleased to have such a skilled artisan in his court. 'Your reputation precedes you, my dear Biru Kalkuda, and I am honoured to have you working in my kingdom,' he exclaimed.

Kalkuda, however, hesitated. 'But my lord, how can I work without my hand and leg?' he asked, a hint of despair creeping into his voice.

But Timmanna Ajila would not be deterred. 'Fear not, my friend,' he assured Kalkuda. 'I shall summon other masons, and you can impart your knowledge to them.'

But Kalkuda was determined to prove his worth. Ignoring his physical limitations, he picked up his chisel and began working on a basadi and Gomata statue. And, to the amazement of all who watched him, he crafted a statue even taller and grander than the one he had made in Karkala.

The sound of stones clattering was heard in Karkala. Bhairavarasu got furious and he sent for people to kill Kalkuda who had dared to carve a structure in another kingdom. In grief and rage, Kalkuda went to a Mahadeva temple and pleaded, 'O Mahadeva! What justice is this? First, I had to long to see my father, then I had to see him dying in front of my eyes, now these people in power are after my life. Above all, my eyes are yearning to see my dear sister who must have grown up now.'

Chapter 5 — Kallamma

That night, Kallamma had a dream in which she saw her brother in dire straits. She could no longer bear to be separated from her brother. 'It has been far too long since I have seen him,' she lamented to her mother. 'I must go in search of him, wherever he may be.'

And so, Kallamma set out on a journey, tracing the same path that her father and brother had taken. She cooked many things, packed them for the journey. She prepared savouries that she wished to share with her dear brother. She travelled to Belur, where she learned that a man named Biru Kalkuda had passed through on his way to Belagola. From there, she followed his trail to Yernad, and then on to Kolluru. Finally, she arrived in Karkala, only to hear of the unspeakable cruelty that had been inflicted upon her beloved brother.

Overcome with grief and despair, Kallamma broke down in tears. But just as she was about to give up hope, a passerby informed her that Biru Kalkuda was now working in the kingdom of Venur. Determined to see her brother once more, Kallamma gathered her strength and continued on her journey.

Finally, after a long and arduous journey, Kallamma arrived in Venur, where she found Kalkuda working on the statue of Gomata. Overcome with emotion, she dropped the parcel of food she had carried and ran to embrace her brother, tears streaming down her face. She identified him because he had one hand and leg missing, but he could not identify his grown-up sister.

Kalkuda, upon noticing the beautiful young Kallamma, asked, 'Who are you?'

'I am Kallamma, your sister. I came because my eyes were yearning to see you, my ears were yearning to hear your voice, and my arms were aching to hold you in embrace, my brother,' she revealed.

They sat together, reunited at last. She knew that nothing could ever break the unbreakable bond between them. As she looked upon his missing limb and hand, her heart filled with sadness. 'Oh, my dear brother,' she said, 'was this punishment for some misdeed or crime?'

But Kalkuda reassured her, 'No, my sister. I was not punished for any misdeed or crime. Bhairavarasu of Karkala gifted this fate upon me so that I could not replicate the work I did in his kingdom anywhere else.'

Despite his injuries, Kalkuda had continued to work and had even surpassed his previous achievements. Kallamma marvelled at the magnificent statue that her brother had created and felt a sense of pride and awe, but at the same time an unquenchable fire was raging within her. With a fierce determination burning in her eyes, Kallamma rose to her feet and proclaimed, 'I shall not abandon my brother in the face of this injustice. We need not suffer like this.' Her gaze landed on the girdle lying nearby and she commanded, 'Cast aside all your tools into the temple grounds.'

Kalkuda complied with her directive while she removed all her jewellery and flung them into the temple as well. The two siblings then took up five torches and proceeded to circumambulate the temple thrice, bathed in the flickering glow of the flames. At last, she prayed to the deity of the temple, 'Mahadeva! Make us disappear into the realm of maya!'

As if by magic, the siblings disappeared into the sacred realm of spirits. In their ethereal forms, they bathed in the sacred waters of the Kaveri and Ganga before making their way to Tirupati. There, they witnessed the vibrant Anantha Nompu festival and Ranga Puja ceremony. Kallamma adorned her 'spirit body' with holy markings and took hold of a powerful cane known as 'beththa', seeking the blessings of Tirupati Balaji. With renewed strength and determination, the spirits of Kalkuda and Kallamma set off for Karkala, resolved to teach Bhairavarasu a lesson he would never forget.

Chapter 6 — Horror Befalls Karkala

The skies in Karkala were tinted in red, and a great storm was brewing. When the spirits arrived there, Kallamma asked, 'Where is the palace of that king who wronged you? Tell me, my brother.'

Kalkuda led the way and they arrived at the palace.

'In their lofty abodes, where deeds of meanness gleam, the time has come to shatter their pride,' Kallurti remarked and then she drifted into the palace.

The spirits set fire to the king's bed and hid his box of jewels. The kitchen vessels and containers became infested with maggots, while the velvet beds were stained crimson by the lifeless forms of animals and birds. Descending from the vast skies, a torrent of black rocks rained, denting the walls and opulent structures that adorned the landscape, many of which were meticulously erected by the hands of Kalkuda. After sending shivers down the spine of the people in the palace, the spirits ventured out into the town. They set fire to the houses and shops of merchants. Soon, the entire town was burning. Karkala was falling. However, this was just the beginning of the horror, for Kallamma would go on to possess all the men, and Kalkuda would possess all the women in the town. They turned five thousand residents of Karkala mad. One day, they took the king's mother and immersed her in water for the next seven nights.

The king was helpless, he didn't know what to do. He called upon all the wise wizards and skilled exorcists to appear before him in court. 'These spirits have caused chaos in my kingdom, and they have taken my mother. How can I subdue them? Surely, there must be some spell that can work on them?' he implored.

The learned ones shook their heads in dismay. 'Indeed, there are many spells that can tame unruly spirits, but these two seem to be immune to all known enchantments.'

'Then what am I to do?' the king demanded.

'There is a renowned priest (Oilaya/Vailaya. Hoilar in Burnell's MS) in Ubaar (Uppinangady). That priest is a great sorcerer and might have the power to help you with these stubborn spirits who are hell-bent on your destruction.'

Chapter 7 — The Visit

In a small house in Ubaar, a knock on the door interrupted the priest's morning rituals. When he opened the door, a boy handed him a scroll, which contained an urgent message requesting his presence in Karkala. As it was a message from the king, without wasting any time, the priest took a holy bath, dressed up, packed some food, and set out on his journey.

As he arrived at the river which he had to cross, the priest sensed that something strange was happening. Waves rose and fell in the otherwise calm river, and he felt as if someone was following him. He turned around, but there was no one there. Fearing the worst, he prayed and kept moving ahead.

Suddenly, a spirit's (Kallamma's) voice asked him threateningly, 'Will you turn around and acknowledge us, or do you want to be thrown into this river?'

The priest's hair stood on end, and he ran back to his house. He sat on a bronze box that he believed was protected from spirits and felt sorry for not acknowledging them. He besought the spirits and asked, 'O spirits, who are you?'

'I am Kallamma, and with me is my brother Biru Kalkuda,' the woman's voice revealed.

'Why are you following me?' the priest asked.

'We know that King Bhairavarasu has called you to exorcise us, but we won't let you do that,' Kallamma replied.

'Why not?'

'Because we want revenge.'

'For what, may I ask?'

'The evil king sliced my brother's hand and leg so that he may never create a bigger marvel than what he created at the king's region,' Kallamma revealed.

The priest sympathized with their pain but could not let them continue to wreak havoc on innocent people for the sins of the egoistic king. He promised to build a sthana for their worship, cover its roof with tiles, and offer them silver ornaments and flowers. He also promised to ensure that they get their respect in Karkala by performing a feast for them with jewels.

After a bit of caution, Kallamma agreed to the priest's proposal, but only on the condition that he would not use any trickery or treachery on them. She revealed their wishes, which included half a ser of tumbada flower, one ser of white rice, kallu, choona, a cane, a betel leaf, a mundolli of mango tree and the milk of a red-coloured cow.

'I will make sure you get these,' the priest promised. 'Now, go to Karkala and relieve those five thousand people of their madness, and I will make the king fulfil your wishes and restore your honour.'

Kallamma instructed, 'At the kingdom, you should sit in a room and worship us there. Then open your betel-nut bag, and chew on a betel-nut. Then we will come to you as spirits, and you must catch us and place us in a nut and put it inside your bag. Then take us back to Ubaar with you and fulfill the promises you made.'

And so, the priest and the spirits made their way to Karkala to fulfil their duties.

Chapter 8 — Veneration of the Spirits

As the priest entered Bhairavarasu's court, the king breathed a sigh of relief.

'Please rid us of these spirits, and I shall grant you any gift you desire,' the king pleaded.

'I know of your ways, sire. But before I exorcise the spirits, I must demand that you grant me their wishes. You have wronged them, and they desire their honour restored.'

'I shall grant their wishes. Whatever they may be,' the king promised.

The priest began his exorcism by retreating to a room on the eastern side of the palace. He opened his betel-nut bag, placed the nuts on betel leaves, and began to chew on one. Suddenly, the spirits entered the room, and as they moved around, they entered the betel-nuts on the leaves.

As soon as this happened, the supernatural occurrences in Karkala ceased, and the people were freed from the madness that had overtaken them. Even the king's mother emerged from the waters, unharmed. The king kept his promise, and the priest returned to Ubaar with the spirits, fulfilling his promise to them.

'We will never forget what you did for us,' the spirits said. 'From now on, we will follow you wherever you go.'

And so, the priest accepted (Satyamma) Kallurti and (Beera) Kalkuda as his guardian spirits. Kallurti and Kalkuda are known for representing truth and justice and are powerful daivas worshipped throughout Tulu Nadu.

Notes

Variations in the Folktale

In certain narratives, the priest, en route to Karkala, encounters a river and a lone boat. The boatman refuses passage, prompting the spirits to assume human form and request the boatman, who remains unyielding. The angered spirits capsize the boat, leading to the boatman's demise. Displaying magical prowess, the spirits transport the priest on an elongated banana leaf, buoyant on the river's surface. Villagers notice the missing boatman and, upon learning of the spirits, beseech their release. The spirits consent, imposing a condition that the boatman must perform kola for forty-eight days. However, after five days, the boatman, apprehensive of the spirits, concocts a plan to end the arrangement by poisoning the chicken curry intended for the impersonator (kola dancer possessed by the spirit). Unexpectedly, the possessed impersonator instructs the boatman to consume the curry, leading to his demise. In some renditions, the boatman's children partake in the poisoned food, losing consciousness. The daiva intervenes, preventing their demise but compelling the boatman to confess his wrongdoing.

In an alternate version of the same tale, when confronted by formidable spirits, the priest decides against proceeding to Karkala. Thus, the kingdom continues to be wrecked by chaos. Meanwhile, the boatman retains his name. In this version, the spirits appear before elu Uduperu (seven priests from Udupi), who, without resistance, acknowledge the spirit deity and submit to her. These priests become carriers of the spirit's glory across the region. Bhairavarasu eventually learns of these spirits. Since the spirits remain displeased in this version, the misfortunes in Karkala persist. Bhairavarasu, setting aside his pride, seeks forgiveness, and the spirit deities receive due respect and veneration.

Karkala, Basadis & the Black Granite

The town of Karkala holds significant geographical importance within the narrative of Kalkuda and Kallurti. Its name, 'Karkala,' is believed to derive from 'Kari Kallu Sthala,' signifying the place of black stone, particularly granite. Renowned as a pivotal pilgrimage destination for Jains, the term 'basadi' finds frequent mention in this story, representing a shrine or place of worship for the Jain community in Karnataka. Interestingly, the word 'basadi' isn't prevalent in the northern regions, but a similar term can be found in the renowned Dilwara Jain temples of Rajasthan, where it is referred to as 'vasahi,' possibly rooted in the Sanskrit word 'vasati.'

The symbolic importance of black rock doesn't end here. The faces of kola dancers who impersonate Kalkuda are painted in shades of darkest black. This echoes the very stone upon which Kalkuda's labour was once devoted. It links the spirit's connection with the earth, an acknowledgement of its origins rooted in the elemental forces of creation. Countless white dots adorn the faces of those impersonating Kallurti and Kalkuda, punctuating the ebony expanse with their luminescent presence. These dots, imbued with symbolic significance, embody the mark left when a stone is struck by an axe.

Because she had set the palace on fire, Kallurti may also be called as Tookatheri by some. In many places, Kallurti is venerated with Panjurli. When the kola artist stands before the awestruck devotees, the convergence of beauty and power becomes palpable. The saree-clad Kallurti and the black-faced Kalkuda, marked by the divine strokes of their artistry, symbolize the delicate interplay of light and darkness, creation and destruction, that underpins the cosmic order.

2

Panjurli—The Boar Deity

THE WORSHIP OF PANJURLI, PERHAPS THE MOST powerful and popular spirit deity in Tulu Nadu, is an age-old tradition whose origin is now shrouded in mystery. The historical proof of its antiquity is manifested in the absence of its genesis story, a tale now lost to time. Currently, the available versions of the story are veiled by the influences of Vaishnavaite or Shaivaite doctrines. As delineated in the section on 'types of daivas', Panjurli is a totemistic deity, represented by the untamed wild boar. The term 'Panji' means boar in Tulu. The other half of the word could be 'Kurli' which means an offspring. Thus, Panjurli may be defined as the offspring of a wild boar.

Panjurli's significance lies in its totemic symbolism, where the boar serves as its emblem. The Vijayanagara empire, which had influence over Tulu Nadu once, carried the regal insignia of an enigmatic allure with an unmistakable peculiarity: the depiction of a boar. A divergence from the conventional Indian emblems of antiquity, the boar assumes a position of prominence, despite its humble origins in Hindu mythology. As we delve deeper into divine lore, we encounter the third avatar, or incarnation, of Lord Vishnu, known as Varaha. This celestial embodiment manifests in the form of a boar, a visual representation that might bewilder the uninitiated. Yet, within the intricate narratives of Hinduism, Varaha assumes a revered place as a Vaishnava icon, embodying a transformative power that defies mundane interpretations. Varaha, in his divine splendour, emerged from the depths of the boundless ocean, resolute in his mission to lift the Earth from its submerged abyss.

Anthropologically speaking, the wild boar is a totem. This attachment to the totem may have originated from ancestral experiences, where a forefather had either favourable or unfavourable encounters with a specific animal or natural object. These experiences could have led them to decree that their descendants should hold respect for the entire species of that particular animal. Based on this, it could be deduced that when humans first started cultivating farmlands, wild boars ravaged their crops. To mitigate the damage caused by these wild beasts, early humans must have resorted to worshipping a spirit that represented the boar. Over time, this spirit deity gained a following and its worship gradually expanded beyond settlements and villages, traversing geographical boundaries. It is possible that both Varaha and Panjurli evolved from the same totem and later on, due to cultural exchange, found some similarities.

Despite its murky origins, the present-day Panjurli has spread to every nook and cranny of Tulu Nadu, becoming intrinsically linked with local legends and folklore. Its divinity has transcended the linguistic barriers, crossed over to the entire country, finding a place in the hearts of every individual who has witnessed the movie, *Kantara*. However, this widespread recognition also spawned controversies surrounding the deity's origin. The song

'Varaha Roopam' created a stir when it equated Panjurli with the Varaha avatar of Lord Vishnu. Whether Panjurli evolved from Varaha or the former inspired the latter is a debate that may never find an answer and keep some occupied, but the mighty groans of Panjurli daiva echoes throughout Tulu Nadu.

Here, I offer two accounts that offer mythological origin stories of this revered spirit deity with the countenance of a boar.

Story 1—Parvati's Dilemma

Once upon a time, in a far-off land, there lived a boar who was as dark as the night and a sow who was as fair as snow. These two soulmates longed to offer their worship to the great deities Ishvara (Shiva) or Narayana at their sacred abodes. Alas, they were plagued by apprehension that the attendants of the lords might not extend a warm welcome to them.

One day, the intrepid couple mustered the courage to venture forth to seek the blessings of Subbramanya, the lord of snakes. Descending the ghats, they bathed their bodies in the cool, purifying waters and arrived at the abode of the deity. With a sense of great humility, they beseeched, 'O Lord, please bestow your blessings upon us, for we have come from the ghats to seek your permission to unite in holy matrimony.'

Lord Subbramanya blessed them, saying, 'So be it, my dear ones. You may now become husband and wife.'

And so it came to pass that the couple descended the ghats, and in time, the female boar became pregnant. By the time they arrived in the plains, she was already seven months along; her body changed and was marked by the ravages of pregnancy. She craved yams (kene), which her mate diligently procured for her. Yet, the consequences of their indulgence in this craving led to the destruction of crops and gardens.

One day, while her mate was away, the sow went into labour. She dug a pit and settled in, gritting her teeth as the pangs of childbirth overtook her. Her moans of pain resounded through the air of all three worlds, Aakaasha, Pataala and Bhumi. Finally, she gave birth to her little ones and ventured down the ghats with them.

One fateful night, the sow and the boar wandered into the garden of Ishvara, where they wreaked havoc upon the flowers, creepers, and all things that were carefully tended and maintained. After their misadventure, they returned to the forest. When Ishvara awoke the next morning, he was crestfallen to see the state of his once-beautiful garden. He immediately called for his attendants and demanded, 'Who has committed this heinous act?'

'It must be some wild beast, O Lord of Lords!' the attendants chorused.

'Then find it!' he ordered.

The attendants searched high and low throughout the forest, until they finally found the sow and boar nestled under a tree. They killed the couple and then called Ishvara. Upon noticing the orphaned piglets, he was struck with compassion and instructed his attendants to bring them to his abode.

At that time, Ishvara's consort, Parvati, had no children of her own. Ishvara implored her, 'Dear Parvati, as you have no children, I request you to raise these piglets as your own.'

'Thank you, my dear Lord. I will nurture them with great love and care,' replied Parvati, overjoyed at the prospect of motherhood.

However, the piglets grew up quickly and found it challenging to restrain their wild and destructive habits. They frequently ravaged Ishvara's garden, and one day, the lord could no longer contain his fury. With a heart full of wrath, he cursed, 'Those wretched little ones! I shall no longer tolerate their behavior. I am going to destroy them all!'

Hearing this, Parvati was filled with immense sorrow. She loved the piglets as though they were her own and implored her husband, 'Please, do not kill them.'

As Parvati pleaded with her husband, Ishvara's fury gradually abated. However, his wrath was not entirely placated, and he still sought to punish the piglets for their misdeeds. After a moment of contemplation, he uttered a curse upon the hapless creatures.

'Very well,' Ishvara said at last, his voice heavy with anger. 'I will spare their lives, but they cannot remain as they are. They shall ascend to the spirit realm as Panjurli, and from there they shall descend to earth, seeking tribute from the people who live there.'

Thus, the spirits of the piglets became Panjurli and arrived on earth.

Notes

This narrative is a retelling of an origin story that was first translated by AC Burnell from Dr Mogling's Kannada manuscript. The original text indicated that Parvati had no children, which is an intriguing detail, given that many of us have grown up hearing stories of her sons Ganesha and Subbramanya. To account for this, I have taken some creative liberty and shifted the focus to a time when Parvati had no children at her abode, either before they were born or after her sons left Kailasa. However, the mention that the boar and sow prayed to Subbramanya, who was the first born of Parvati, contradicts the former theory.

A fascinating facet of this ancient tale is the possibility of it holding a deeper social commentary beyond its mystical elements. Upon examining the narrative, one may theorise that the character Ishvara could have been based on a high-ranking individual in the region who was without progeny.

Story 2—The Fearsome Spirit

One day, Brahma paid a visit to Vishnu at his celestial abode, Vaikuntha. Meanwhile, the vigilant gatekeepers, Jaya and Vijaya, maintained their watchful stance outside the entrance. Just as always, they observed the infinite ocean of milk tenderly cradling everything within its vast embrace. Abruptly, the ground beneath them trembled, and the distant echoes of trumpets and drums reverberated in the air. The ocean waters responded with ripples as a group of bhuta-ganas from Kailasa approached the gates of Vaikuntha. Leading this celestial entourage were none other than the Supreme Lord, Ishvara, accompanied by his cherished consort Parvati, gracefully mounted atop Nandi, the divine bull.

'O Vijaya, who is this coming with such grandeur?' inquired Jaya.

Vijaya looked ahead and saw the bhuta-gana, and in the centre was Shiva and Parvati. 'It is Ishvara, the lord of the universe, coming to visit the lord of all universes, Narayana,' Vijaya replied.

'But why is there such a commotion?' asked Jaya.

'Oh! Ishvara is coming with his entire bhuta-gana,' said Vijaya.

'All sixty-four thousand of them?' Jaya exclaimed.

'Yes,' Vijaya confirmed.

The gates of Vaikuntha opened for Ishvara and his gang, and they were warmly welcomed inside by Jaya and Vijaya. The lord of lords joined Brahma, and they commenced discussing the fate of their creations. As their conversation went on, the presence of so many bhuta-ganas raised the temperature of Vaikuntha. Mists ascended from the expanse of the primeval waters, where Narayana resided. At one point, Narayana started to perspire, and he scratched his arm, causing a drop of sweat to fall on earth. As soon as it touched the soil, it started to fume, and when the fumes subsided, a great boar revealed itself. The boar ran amok, and anyone who got in its way was driven away.

Ishvara, Brahma and the bhuta-ganas watched in wonderment from Vaikuntha.

'What is this creation, Narayana?' the bhuta-ganas inquired.

Narayana, the divine preserver of the universe, smiled serenely, his gaze fixed on the great boar. The creature roared and struck the earth with its mighty tusks, its massive form shaking the very foundations of Vaikuntha, the celestial abode of Lord Narayana. As the bhuta-ganas from Kailasa watched in awe, Narayana explained the boar's origins.

'Just like this ocean is brimming with tiny droplets of water, the earth we created was brimming with sinners,' he said. 'And so, I willingly orchestrated the creation of this great boar out of my sweat. I have sent it down to trouble the sinners in order to make them humble and wise.'

As if on cue, the great boar rose from the depths of the ocean and entered Vaikuntha. Its massive form was illuminated by a beam of golden light that streamed down from the heavens above. Its eyes glowed with a fierce intensity, and its muscles rippled with power as it stood before the Trinity (Trimurti), trembling with anger and vigour.

The surrounding waters churned and roiled, as though the very elements of the Vaikuntha were responding to the creature's presence. The sky overhead darkened, and the wind began to howl, carrying with it a sense of awe and wonder. Ishvara and Parvati, Brahma and the bhuta-gana were spellbound, for they had never seen such a magnificent beast before. The creature's thick fur shone like burnished gold in the light of the sun, and its tusks gleamed like polished ivory.

As the creature approached Narayana, the ground shook with each heavy footstep, causing the nearby waves to sway and bend. The air was filled with the sound of crashing waves and the roar of the beast's mighty breaths.

'Behold, Ishvara and Brahma,' said Narayana, 'this boar cannot speak, and here it has come so that I could give him the gift of speech. However, before I give him this gift I will, for a moment, reveal his true form before your eyes.'

Narayana held the boar by the tusk and flicked the boar away; it flew through the air before landing gracefully on the surface of the great ocean. The boar began to transform into a human, growing in size until it towered over the surrounding waves like a giant coconut palm. Its arrival caused a great commotion among the bhuta-ganas who were present there. They hadn't witnessed anything like that before.

Ishvara, Brahma and the bhuta-ganas stood in awe at the sight before them, marvelling at the creature that Narayana had created. They praised Narayana for his infinite power and creativity, recognizing that he was the one who had created not just this magnificent boar but also humankind and the eighty-four lakhs of animals and birds on earth.

As the boar trembled in its newfound giant human form, it approached Narayana, seeking guidance.

'Speak now, what is it that you seek?' commanded Narayana, his voice booming like thunder.

The boar in its gigantic human form prostrated before the lord and revealed its thirst. 'O Narayana, I am thirsty,' it said. 'I cannot control this thirst. My throat has dried up. Show me a way to quench my thirst. If I am to live then I must quench this thirst first.'

Narayana, with his infinite wisdom, knew exactly what to do.

'You may drink as much as you want from the deva-pushkarani (holy pond),' he replied.

With gratitude in its heart, the boar in human form obediently followed Narayana's instruction, lowering its massive head into the shimmering waters of the celestial pond and drinking deeply. As it drank, it could feel the cool water revitalizing its parched throat.

But as the giant raised its head and turned to face Narayana once more, it could feel another hunger gnawing at its belly. 'O Lord, my thirst is now quenched,' it said. 'But now I am hungry. What do I do? I cannot control this hunger, O Lord! Show me a way to obtain food.'

In the grand celestial world of Vaikuntha, Lord Narayana gazed upon the magnificent creation before him, born from the sweat of his own divine body. He smiled benevolently at it, recognizing it as his own son. 'Behold!' he exclaimed. 'You are my own creation, and I shall heed your every request. It would be a great shame otherwise.'

The boar in human form eagerly awaited its next command. 'Tell me, O Lord,' it implored.

'I know your hunger,' Lord Narayana acknowledged. 'To satiate your craving, you must go to the earth below in your spirit form, where there are many sinners who cherish their children, crops, and cattle. You must take the form of the boar and enter their cattle sheds to attack their animals.'

The boar in human form obediently agreed, eager to please his divine father. But then it voiced a concern. 'But how will I obtain my food? Do I eat those cattle?' it asked.

'No,' Lord Narayana said and smiled serenely. 'When tragedy befall such wicked humans, they shall worship you and feed you. You can possess the body of a human and consume whatever you feel like—flesh, tender coconuts, beaten rice, jaggery and sugarcane.'

Overwhelmed with joy, the boar in human form leaped into the air, causing great waves to crash against the primeval ocean. However, a sudden doubt sprang up in its mind. 'But, O Lord,' it queried, 'when I possess the body of a human and make them tremble, what shall I tell them when they ask me who I am? What is my name?'

With great pomp and grandeur, Lord Narayana replied, 'Establish your name in the world of humans and receive tributes, and be happy. Henceforth, your name shall be ... Panjurli!'

Notes

What is particularly fascinating about this tale is how it bears resemblance to 'The Origin of Bhutas', in which spirit deities are dispatched to Earth to punish sinners. The difference here is that it is Vishnu, rather than Shiva, who sends the creation of his sweat from Vaikuntha, as opposed to Shiva's ganda-ganas from Kailasa. Nonetheless, there are similarities in the two accounts of Panjurli's origin. In the first (titled 'Parvati's Dilemma'), Shiva exiles the boar to Earth, and before descending the ghats, the sow and boar receive blessings from Subbramanya. Similarly, here Panjurli is delegated to Earth by Vishnu, and the spirit first seeks blessings from Subbramanya before embarking on his descent down the ghats. The next story is a continuation of the previous one. It narrates the arrival of the spirit deity onto the earthly realm. A common motif among folk beliefs pertaining to such spirits is their inclination to manifest miracles at a specific location before embarking on a journey to the next, often by following a person or latching on to their backs - a term that is locally known as beri pasthu barpuna.

Story 3 — Panjurli's Arrival

Panjurli in the spirit form wandered across the many paths that led to earth. With an unwavering focus on his mission, he chose the one that led him to the ghats, and descended them with a determined stride. Seven days and as many nights he roamed before arriving at the abode of Subbramanya. Here, he bowed before the lord of snakes and prayed for his grace. And then, in a miraculous moment, the temple bell rang on its own, which he took as an auspicious sign. Fuelled by newfound confidence, he set forth towards his ultimate destination.

It was in the forest at Mardala where he first caught sight of a manor house, with its ornate architecture and beguiling beauty. He could sense an air of pride emanating from the house. A great hunger seized him, and he longed for a feast fit for a deity. And so he resolved to enter the house and claim his due, spreading his name far and wide in the process.

As the sun blazed overhead, Panjurli circled the mansion in the guise of a gentle breeze. He studied the people who lived inside and the cattle that grazed outside. It was the sight of the plump cows and stout oxen that spurred him to action. And so, with the onset of dusk, he made his move.

Stealthily, he entered the cow shed and waited in a corner, watching as the cowherds finished their chores and locked up the shed for the night. Once the boys had gone for dinner, Panjurli struck with a speed and agility that only a supernatural entity could possess.

Everyone was fast asleep, but in the middle of the night, the oxen that raced in the kambala, clumsily moved from its place. The master of the house, a proud Ballal, who was sleeping on a swinging cot, heard coughs from the shed. He awoke his wife and said, 'Did you hear them?'

The wife also heard the commotion amidst the whistling of a wild wind.

'Quick! Light a lamp and hand it to me,' the master instructed his wife.

As the night deepened, the darkness outside the cowshed only grew more intense, and the only light that illuminated the area was a flickering lamp held by the master Ballal. He was closely followed by his nephew, Ishara. The shadows of the oxen were cast in strange, contorted shapes on the walls, and their horns appeared even more menacing in the dim light, giving the impression of a horde of fearsome rakshasas lurking in the corners.

As they stepped inside, the stench of sickness and decay hung heavy in the air, making it difficult for the master and his nephew to breathe. The oxen lay prostrate on the ground, their bodies wracked with pain and their eyes filled with an unexplainable terror. Their legs were weak and could barely support their weight. The master and his nephew were both taken aback, for the animals had been in perfect health only a few hours before.

'What could have caused this?' the master asked, his voice filled with dread.

'I cannot say,' the nephew replied, his voice low and trembling.

As they turned to leave, the buffaloes and cows began to wheeze and choke, their breaths coming in short, rasping gasps. The master and his nephew knew that they could do nothing at that hour of the night, so they left the shed with heavy hearts, feeling helpless and defeated.

As morning arrived, the news of the sick cattle had spread, and the neighbours began to arrive one by one, observing the animals in silence. It was clear that something sinister was at play, for the cows were foaming at the mouth and writhing in agony.

'It must be the work of a spirit,' one of the neighbours said, speaking for all.

The master was filled with a sense of dread, for he knew that he was dealing with a power beyond his understanding. He turned to the neighbours, hoping for some guidance.

'What do I do now?' he asked, his voice tinged with desperation.

'We suggest you consult an astrologer,' one of the neighbours replied. 'Perhaps he can tell you what to do.'

The master Ballal arrived with an offering of coconuts at the doorstep of Bhatta, a learned astrologer. The air was thick with an ominous aura, as if something dark loomed on the horizon. The master stood patiently in the verandah, waiting for Bhatta to conclude his morning rituals. When the astrologer emerged, the master greeted him with folded hands and asked for his counsel.

'O Bhatta, something grave has occurred at my homestead. My oxen and cows are afflicted with an unknown ailment. No medicine can cure them, and I fear for their lives. Please, I implore you, help me in this time of need,' the master Ballal beseeched the astrologer.

Bhatta nodded sagely and led the master inside. He retrieved a box of cowrie shells and arranged them in twelve piles on a wooden board, one for each sign of the zodiac. Then, with closed eyes, he prayed to the planetary gods and sought their guidance.

'O Narayana, reveal to us the truth behind this man's affliction,' Bhatta intoned. He opened his eyes and instructed the master to place a coin as dakshina (fee) before each pile of shells.

Bhatta scrutinized the shells with a furrowed brow, as if he were deciphering an inscrutable code.

'You are beset by a new spirit who was not present in your house or this land before,' Bhatta declared. Looking at the board, he added, 'Since you placed your dakshina on *mesha*, I assume that this spirit has the face of a boar, and it demands a sacrifice and a feast. Furthermore, it desires a sthaana near your dwelling, where it can receive offerings.'

The master was taken aback. 'A boar? What manner of spirit is this?' he asked.

Bhatta shook his head gravely and said, 'It is not for us mortals to understand the ways of the spirit deities. But I can tell you this much; if you construct a sthaana as it demands, it will leave you and your livestock in peace.'

The master was quick to assent. He said, 'I will build the sthaana, as you suggest. But first, I must tend to my cattle. Will this spirit heal them as well?'

Bhatta closed his eyes once more and prayed for a sign of good fortune. He examined the shells once again and smiled. 'Yes, the spirit will cure your cattle. In fact, when you return home, they will be restored to health.'

The master was overjoyed. But he had one last question for Bhatta. 'When should I construct the sthaana? Please give me an auspicious date.'

Bhatta sighed wearily. 'Who am I to give you a date? Understand. The daiva that has arrived at your house, his name is Panjurli. Mind you, he is not a minor deity. It will not be easy to placate him. You must first find a suitable host for the spirit to possess. Only then should you begin the construction of the sthaana, on a day that the spirit itself designates.'

'And when is an auspicious day to invoke the spirit into a host's body?' the master asked eagerly.

Bhatta consulted his almanac and pronounced, 'Friday, the twenty-seventh, is an auspicious day.'

'You must be present, Bhatta,' the master insisted.

Bhatta hesitated. 'I have young children to tend to. What could I possibly do at the sthaana?'

Before they could continue their discussion, Ishara, the nephew of the master, burst into the room. 'Uncle, a miracle has occurred! The oxen have risen to their feet, and the cows have stopped gasping! Now you must come home as aunty has prepared our meals.'

The master Ballal and Bhatta exchanged a knowing glance. 'I told you it was Panjurli,' the astrologer said with conviction. 'Now, you must do as it commands.'

Saying thus, the astrologer left for a temple, and the master and his nephew returned to their house.

As the master of the house returned from the astrologer's place, he immediately made his way to the shed to check on his beloved cattle. Overwhelmed with joy at the sight of his livestock in good health, he made his way towards the chavadi, where he encountered his dear wife.

'My love, are you not hungry? The meal I had prepared with such care and attention has now gone cold,' his wife inquired.

This question provoked the proud master, who furrowed his brow and snapped, 'Are you lamenting over the meal that is already cooked? Is that all that concerns you?'

His wife began to reply, but was cut off by her husband's curt tone. 'Go and check on the oxen and cows in the shed. My swift action and visit to the astrologer have brought them back to good health. As long as they are alive, we have sustenance. What would you know? The moment they fell ill, hunger and thirst disappeared from my mind.'

As if on cue, the nephew came running to the chavadi, rubbing his belly in hunger. 'Oh, dear aunty, I am famished. Please serve me some food,' he implored.

This sight only served to further enrage the master, who spat at his nephew, 'You are of no use to us, yet you take advantage of the food we give you.'

The boy, confused and hurt by his uncle's outburst, implored, 'Forgive me, uncle. But why are you scolding me? Aren't you supposed to be happy?'

'I am scolding you because even after coming to the astrologer's house and witnessing the swift recovery of our cattle, you didn't even bother to ask what caused their illness. You didn't even care to know how your uncle's quick actions saved our precious livestock,' he retorted, his voice laced with anger.

'I was going to ask, but then I became so famished that I forgot,' the boy responded.

'Always thinking about your next meal, you silly one,' his uncle chided, causing Ishara to hang his head in shame.

After rebuking his nephew, the master retired to his quarters for the much-needed respite. Then the master settled down to eat his meal with his nephew. His chest swelled with pride as he recounted the story of Panjurli, the powerful spirit who had brought disease upon his cattle. With an air of self-importance, he declared that it was now his duty to construct a sthaana for the daiva, for who else but he was capable of such a feat? His voice boomed with confidence as he spoke, and those around him could not help but be impressed by his unwavering resolve.

The master of the house summoned a vaastu expert to seek counsel on where to erect the sthaana for the daiva. After a thorough walk around the land, the expert pointed out a spot near a majestic banyan tree.

'This is the perfect location. Your sthaana must be built here,' the expert declared confidently.

But the master was quick to interject with a hint of condescension in his voice, 'And do you think the mere utterance of words would bring the sthaana to life?'

The expert, sensing the master's pride, replied humbly, 'No, sir. We must take measurements and carry out the construction process.'

'Exactly my point! Waste no time, bring your instruments and measure the ground at once!' the master commanded with fervour.

On the following Friday, the woodcutters were summoned to fell trees, as the master had requested. They worked hard until the sun reached its zenith and the heat became unbearable, causing their throats to dry up and their eyes to blur.

The master scolded them for their lack of endurance, saying, 'What kind of men are you? A single day's work has exhausted you! You must finish everything before the sun sets today. Tomorrow, the carpenters will come and you must have erected four posts upon which the trees will be sawn.'

The woodcutters hastened their efforts, but soon faced another obstacle. 'Master,' they said, 'we cannot find any suitable trees for your work. We must go farther from the village to find one.'

'Very well,' said the master.

And so, they journeyed eastward until they came upon a colossal tree. As they approached the towering tree, a sense of foreboding began to take hold of them. The gnarled roots of the gigantic tree seemed to be clawing at the earth, while its branches stretched up to the heavens as if reaching for the gods themselves. The skies turned red, and a palpable sense of otherworldliness emanated from the tree. The woodcutters were filled with fear.

'Here is a big tree,' said the master, 'which I hope will suffice.'

As they stood next to the tree with their axes, dark red clouds began to swirl in the sky above. The wind began to pick up, howling through the trees, and a sense of dread filled the air. The woodcutters hesitated, sensing that they had angered some daiva in the sacred realm of spirits.

'We should not cut this tree,' the woodcutters declared in unison.

'Why not?' asked the master.

'Master, we have built temples, mathas, shrines and sthaanas. We have cut down large trees for these purposes. But we feel that this particular tree should not be felled. When we look at it, our heads spin. You should consult someone before cutting it down.'

'You boast of cutting down big trees for temples and shrines,' said the master, 'but now you tremble like wet cats. If I tell others, they will laugh at you and never hire you again.'

'Master,' they pleaded, 'we implore you not to cut this tree. There seems to be a miracle or a spirit associated with it. If you fell it without consulting someone, the spirit will be angered.'

'Fell the tree,' said the master, 'and I shall bear the consequences.'

One of the woodcutters, named Karagachari, picked up his axe and was about to strike the tree when he suddenly threw it away and began to shake uncontrollably. The sky grew darker until it was the colour of black granite, and occasional lightning illuminated the face of the woodcutter, who was now possessed by a daiva.

'O Karagachari!' called out the master, ignoring the sudden change in the weather.

'Do not call him,' warned the other woodcutters. 'He is possessed by a spirit. There seems to be a miracle associated with this tree. We told you to consult someone before felling it. Now the daiva will speak through this possessed man.'

As the air thickened with a foreboding sense of doom, the possessed Karagachari, his eyes ablaze with an otherworldly fire, shattered his axe and began to beat his chest and belly with the jagged handle. His cries rent the air, carrying with them the force of the supernatural.

The woodcutters, their voices shaking with fear, implored the spirit to reveal its true identity. 'We beseech you,' they cried, 'if you are the embodiment of satya and righteousness, then tell us who you are and why you have chosen to afflict our comrade with such pain. How can he continue to toil for his livelihood if you render him limbless?'

With a voice like thunder, the spirit that had taken possession of the man spoke out. 'Ballal, you have come here with these men, seeking to fell this tree which is my home. I know why you did this. I am aware of Panjurli, for he is my friend. Seek another tree elsewhere, to the north, where you will find many suitable for Panjurli's sthaana. And since you asked, know that my name is Kallurti. Now, leave this place, for I shall soon release this man from my grasp.'

Ballal quickly opened a tender coconut and offered it to the possessed Karagachari, who drank deeply from it. The coconut fell to the ground with a thud, as did the man, as if he were shedding the spirit that had taken over his being. The dark clouds that had gathered in the sky dispersed, and the warm orange light of dusk flooded the forest floor.

Moments later, Karagachari regained consciousness, looking around in confusion. 'Master,' he asked Ballal, 'why have we not yet felled this tree? Is it not getting late?'

The woodcutters and Ballal exchanged uneasy glances. 'Do you not remember what happened to you?' they asked.

Karagachari shook his head. 'No, I do not recall. My head felt dizzy, and then I knew nothing. But now my body aches, as if I have been beaten. What happened to me?'

The woodcutters explained what had transpired, and the group quickly left for the north, where they found suitable trees and felled them with alacrity, and hurried back to their homes, eager to put that terrifying encounter with Kallurti behind them.

In this state of mind, Ballal realized how small and insignificant he was in the grand scheme of things. He saw that there were forces beyond his control, powers that could crush him in an instant if they chose to. He began to see the world with new eyes, as if it were a vast, dangerous wilderness filled with perils at every turn.

As the construction of the sthaana progressed, a transformation also took hold of Ballal. His once critical nature vanished, replaced by a newfound sense of empathy and understanding towards others. He had come to realize that everyone had their own struggles to bear, and it was not his place to judge them.

With the sthaana almost completed, Ballal made his way to the astrologer, seeking an auspicious date to dedicate the structure to Panjurli daiva. The astrologer, well-versed in the cosmic rhythms and movements of the celestial bodies, quickly picked a date and time that was deemed favourable to the daiva. Ballal also made arrangements to invite a kola dancer, as an embodiment of the spirit of Panjurli.

On the auspicious day, the astrologer conducted the necessary rituals, and the kola dancer began to spin and move, his body contorting in a rhythmic dance. Many people had also assembled.

'O Lord Panjurli, if you are the spirit of truth and justice, reveal yourself to us,' Ballal beseeched the kola dancer.

Above him, the clouds began to collect and swirl in a similar pattern.

'Please come down from the skies, and enter this sthana ... Please come out of the sthaana and enter this human ... O Panjurli, spirit of truth!' Ballal entreated.

Suddenly, a ray of light burst forth from the swirling clouds, illuminating the dancer's body. And from the sacred realm of maya, the spirit of Panjurli descended upon the dancer's form, taking possession of him.

With his legs trembling rhythmically, the kola dancer began to speak in a voice not his own. 'O Ballal, I am Panjurli, the spirit of truth and justice. I came down from the sky without needing a ladder. I have seen the devotion you have shown me and I am extremely elated. But you must not forget me, and send offerings twice every year. If you fail, then I will make sure to give you trouble. Do not complain like you used to complain all the time.'

With humility, Ballal responded, 'I will do as you ask, O Panjurli.'

'I am pleased to hear that,' the spirit replied. 'As long as you offer me your devotion, I will ensure that no disease befalls your cattle or children. Now, bring me food and milk, for this human body that I have possessed is growing weary. After that, I will move on to the next town, seeking offerings to quench my hunger and thirst.'

As Ballal made offerings of food and the customary glass of milk, Panjurli feasted heartily. Once he had eaten his fill, he left the body of the kola dancer, and the assembly of people slowly dispersed. As Ballal watched the last of the villagers depart, he felt a sense of peace and contentment in his heart. He knew that he had done something good, and that the spirit of Panjurli would always watch over him and his family, as long as they showed their devotion.

Notes

This story depicts the journey of a spirit deity once it descends into the earthly realm. During that era, rural life predominated, with cattle rearing constituting a pivotal aspect of households. The spirit deity caused disturbances among cattle, children, or occasionally, older individuals. Seeking resolution, people consulted astrologers proficient in the ancient art of 'prashnam' analysis. Even rural medics or healers in those times believed in such invisible forces of nature. The diagnosis would reveal the involvement of a spirit deity (daiva) or, at times, the spirit of a deceased (preta) causing the disturbances. Remedies ranged from simple acts like illuminating a lamp at a sacred site to orchestrating a kola ceremony.

From a psychological perspective, this may be seen as reflections of the human psyche's attempt to make sense of and cope with the challenges and uncertainties of life. The attribution of disturbances to spirit deities or supernatural forces may serve as a way for individuals to externalize and personify their fears and difficulties. Seeking guidance from oracles or engaging in rituals or visiting religious places could be viewed as mechanisms to regain a sense of control and order in the face of perceived disruptions. However, this is just the rational way to explain things that are beyond the understanding of the ordinary mind.

Let us look at another story which is quite well-known in the region as it is connected to one of the most popular temples of India.

Story 4—Annappa Panjurli

Once upon a time, in the holy land of Dharmasthala, there lived a Pergade. He was suffering from a grave illness, and despite trying all possible medicines and treatments, nothing seemed to cure him.

One day, while his wife was on her way to a shrine, she came across a mendicant on a paddy field. The mendicant pleaded with her, 'O Madam, show your kindness and please give me something to eat.'

But alas! She had nothing on her at that time.

Feeling a little disappointed, she replied, 'Forgive me, but I have nothing with me right now. I am going to a shrine. When I return, if I have something, I shall give you.'

The mendicant thanked her and let her continue on her journey.

After praying at the shrine, she started her journey back home. As she was passing by the same paddy field, she saw that the mendicant was still there, looking weak and hungry. He asked, 'O Madam, show your kindness and please give me something to eat.'

Moved by the mendicant's plight, she went up to him and handed him a prasaada from the shrine and said, 'If you come home, then I can give you some congee.'

'Yes, Madam!' the mendicant said and followed her home.

As promised, she gave him food.

The mendicant noticed that the woman's husband was lying unwell. Curious, the mendicant asked the woman, 'What happened to your husband?'

The woman replied, 'My husband has been unwell for quite some time, and we've tried everything, but nothing has worked. Do you know of any medicine that can cure him?'

The mendicant excused himself and went into the forest to search for some herbs. He returned with the herbs and gave them to the woman.

'I have been applying such herbs for such a long time but they never worked. Why don't you apply it with your hands?' the woman requested.

He applied the herbs to the husband's body. Within minutes, the husband got up and stood on his feet. It was nothing short of a miracle!

Overjoyed, the pergade declared, 'O dear, you may have come here as a stranger, but you have magically cured me. So now, you are like my son. From now on, you will live here. Tell me who you are ...'

The mendicant replied in a riddle, 'I am who I am.'

Little did they know that the mendicant was no ordinary man, but Panjurli, the powerful deity who had taken human form. The mendicant came to be known as Annappa Swamy.

Legend goes that a few days later, the husband had a dream where the Dharmadaivas instructed him to vacate his house and build a shrine for them. He obeyed the command and invited priests to perform the rituals. However, the priests requested him to install a Shivalinga for their worship. He was worried as to how and who would bring a Shivalinga there. Annappa Swamy came forward and offered his help.

Without wasting any time, Annappa Swamy left for Kadri to bring a Shivalinga. When he reached the temple, he tried to take the presiding Shivalinga of Kadri Manjunatha temple, but Lord Shiva spoke from within the Shivalinga and instructed him to take any other linga from his pond. Annappa Swamy flew into the pond in the form of a bee, took the linga, and flew back to the pergade's place.

Notes

I heard this story from Kariya, about whom I have mentioned elsewhere in this book. Annappa Panjurli, Kuppe Panjurli, Baggu Panjurli, Alevara Panjurli, Malara Panjurli, Boti Panjurli, and Angana Panjurli are among the many that have gained prominence over the years. Yet, it is vital to remember that these different forms are not fundamentally distinct entities. Rather, they are but local variations of a larger whole, adapting to the customs and traditions of the communities that embraced them. It could be said that the totem of the boar thus evolved into one of the most venerated deity of the region. The diverse forms of Panjurli may bear different names in different locales, but they are ultimately all linked to the same 'satya' or true spiritual essence, reflecting the many ways in which human culture gives expression to the eternal divine.

3
Koragajja

IN THE UNWRITTEN PAGES OF TULU FOLKLORE, FEW figures loom larger than Koragajja. For the uninitiated, the term 'Koraga' refers to a community that was plagued by the social evil of untouchability, while 'Ajja' connotes an aged man or grandfather in the local language. Yet, it is the melding of these two seemingly disparate elements that gave rise to the moniker 'Koragajja', a figure who is remembered to this day for his boundless affection for children. Many also believe that he got this name because he used to speak like a wise old man despite being of tender age.

Chapter 1—Birth of Taniya

In a remote village nestled amidst lush greenery, resided a couple from the Koraga community whose hearts brimmed with love for each other. The woman bore the fruit of their love, a baby boy called Taniya, on the auspicious ninth day of the ninth month. However, fate proved unkind, as the young mother breathed her last while suckling her newborn. Soon after, the father too passed away, leaving the infant to the care of his community. The boy was raised by his benevolent neighbours, but alas, death claimed them all too soon, leaving the orphaned child bereft of any guardian or company.

The young Taniya, thus, took off on a journey towards the south, braving the scorching heat and traversing many a weary mile, all in search of a purpose to his life. As he walked, he was greeted with either cold glances or utter disregard from those he crossed paths with, but he did not falter, driven by a desperate hunger and thirst for both sustenance and meaning.

Finally, exhausted and on the verge of collapsing, he stopped and decided to invoke Ishvara by offering rice, coconut and betel nut, in the hope of seeking a path to his future. However, he did not have any of those items to offer, so he hatched an innocent plan.

And so it was, that while the boy was lost in prayer, the passers-by could not help but notice him. Naked and clutching a handful of white gritty sand assuming it to be the pearly white rice to be offered to Ishvara, he appeared to be in the throes of a madman's frenzy. He laughed uncontrollably one moment, and the next, he broke down in sobs, and then he would dance like crazy. It was then that a woman by the name of Bairakke Baidyedi happened to chance upon him. Bairakke was carrying a pot of toddy covered with an areca sheath, and had her two young children, Athu and Chinnayya, in tow. Upon seeing the boy, they too were taken aback by his peculiar behaviour.

'What is wrong with that boy?' enquired Bairakke.

'I do not know, mother,' replied Chinnayya.

'But let us go and find out,' Athu said.

And so, they approached the boy, who, upon seeing them, darted away like a frightened deer and hid behind a bush.

'O child!' Bairakke called out to him.

The boy peered out from behind the bush and timidly spoke, 'Yes, mother?'

'Why are you behaving like this, my child?' she asked him.

'I don't know what to do in life, for I have no one in this world to call my own, no home to go back to,' he lamented.

Upon hearing his plight, Bairakke's heart went out to him, and she said, 'Why don't you come to our home?'

'I will come with you, mother, but I have no clothes to wear,' he replied, his voice heavy with shame, 'Would you be kind enough to give me a cap to cover my head and cloth to cover my waist?'

Upon hearing this, Athu and Chinnayya quickly thought of an idea. They unrolled the cloth that was wrapped around the pot containing toddy and gave it to the boy to drape around his waist. Then, they broke the areca leaf sheath that covered the pot into two halves and gave one to him so that he could cover his head. Thus, with his modesty preserved, the boy set off with Bairakke and her children, grateful for their kindness and hospitality. On the way, Koraga Taniya revealed details about his family and put forth his desire to seek a place where he would have plenty of work to do and an abundance of food to eat.

Chapter 2 — Taniya's arrival at Bairakke's Home

When Koraga Taniya arrived at Bairakke's humble home, he seemed to bring along with him a sense of serendipity and felicity. In no time, the family's toddy business began to flourish and prosper, as did their fortunes. Koraga Taniya was a master basket-weaver, and his craftsmanship proved to be an asset that brought them great riches. Driven by his boundless love and compassion, he even fashioned a receptacle for Bairakke to store her toddy. To her amazement, she discovered that the toddy within that specific pot never seemed to run dry, as if by magic. Overwhelmed by curiosity, she inquired of Koraga Taniya what manner of sorcery that was. His simple reply was that she needed only to remove the cloth that had been rolled under the pot, and the toddy would flow out.

One day, a kola dance ritual was to be held at the daivasthaana of the daivas that Bairakke's family worshipped. She was to send offerings of banana, coconut leaves, and 'bonda' (tender coconut) for the kola, but with no one to carry them, she stared forlornly at the strewn items in her front yard.

Filled with a pang of despair, she called out to Koraga Taniya, 'O son, would you be able to take these to the temple for the kola?'

Noticing the heavy load of items, Koraga Taniya replied with concern, 'O mother, these are to be carried by at least seven grown-up men.'

Bairakke sighed, as she pondered the impossibility of the task. But, Taniya was not one to give up easily.

'O mother, I cannot see grief on your face. Why don't you feed me the meal for seven people, then I shall gain the strength to carry this load to the daivasthaana,' he said.

And so, Bairakke served him meals of rice and banguda (Indian mackerel) curry that was meant for seven people. After the heavy meal, his belly protruding in fullness, Koraga Taniya lifted the entire load all by himself and started walking to the temple.

As he stopped on the way, with his back towards Bairakke, he prophesized, 'Farewell, dear mother, I must depart ... from this home, I now must part ... You'll see my back as I walk away ... but my belly, nevermore to display.'

There was something about the boy's demeanour that gave him an unshakeable intuition that he may not return after that day.

Upon reaching outside the temple with the heavy load, the crowd stopped him from entering as his community was not allowed inside the premises at that time. The chief of the temple came forward and commanded Koraga Taniya to place the load on the side and then instructed some boys to take them inside.

'Though my caste may forbid me to come nigh ... these offerings I bring are pure and spry ... the daivas and gods shall consume with grace ... why deny me entry to this holy place?' pleaded the boy, but the chief ignored him. Disappointed, he walked out and stood near a tree. As he looked around, he noticed a citron, which Bairakke loved for pickling, growing on the branches.

Without a second thought, Koraga Taniya climbed the tree and plucked the citron. But, as fate would have it, while climbing, he accidentally stepped on the walls of the temple. The moment his foot touched the stone of the daivasthaana, he vanished into the sacred realm of the spirits. He was never heard of as a human ever again, but soon, the stories of his miracles spread far and wide, and his spirit lived on as a testament to the enduring power of faith and devotion.

Notes

Koraga

The Koraga, designated as a Particularly Vulnerable Tribal Group (PVTG), inhabit the coastal regions of Karnataka and Kerala, numbering around 15,000 as per the 2011 census. Historically, they were renowned for their expertise in basket making, crafting various items such as cradles, paddy cylinders, winnowing and sowing baskets, scale-pans, boxes and more, as echoed in the tale of Koragajja. In the not-so-distant past, they served as slaves on the outskirts of villages, residing in leaf huts known as koppus. They were not allowed to dwell in houses of clay or mud. Some were not even allowed to wear a dress, while others were attired in minimal covering like aprons made of twigs and leaves, iron bracelets and areca-nut spathe caps. They were excluded from entering temples. The story of Koragajja mirrors their historical exclusion from places of worship.

Despite their untouchable status in the past, Koragas identify themselves as Hindus, adhering to a tribal religious system which could have origins in sun worship. They are associated with the names of days like Aita (Aditya, the sun), Toma (Soma, the moon), Angara (Mangala), Gurva (Jupiter), Tanya (Shani, or Saturn), and Tukra (Shukra, or Venus). They have no separate temples for their god, but a place beneath a kāsaracana tree is consecrated for the worship of the deity which is exclusively their own, and is called Kata (Thurston, 1909 page no. 272).

The Mystery of Koragajja's Disappearance

As with many legendary figures of his ilk, the origins of Koragajja's renown are shrouded in mystery. Some claim that his infamy stems from his brazen disregard for the strictures of caste, a transgression that ultimately led to his untimely demise. Others, however, attribute his sudden disappearance to more mystical forces, suggesting that he was spirited away by the very deities he worshipped for committing the 'crime' of entering a temple.

Despite the uncertainty that surrounds his life and death, Koragajja's legacy endures to this day. Indeed, it is said that his kola is a sight to behold, with the artist eschewing the customary 'ani' and instead smearing his body and face with black soot, a powerful symbol of his otherworldly connection. Devotees of Koragajja honour him with chakkulis and a quarter of liquor.

Ultimately, the truth of Koragajja's life may remain forever elusive, lost to the inscrutable realm of maya. Yet, his spirit lives on, being venerated by one and all.

4
Koti Chennaya—The Story of the Warrior Brothers

THE STORY OF KOTI AND CHENNAYA IS ONE OF THE most important folk epics of Tulu Nadu. I have tried to present a very condensed version of this folktale here. To be honest, one book is not enough to portray the valour of the twin brothers.

Chapter 1—The Story of Deyi Baidyadi

One day, when the sun was hidden inside an eclipse, a childless brahmin called Pijanar was taking a bath in the vast sea. At that moment, he came across a lustrous golden egg that had fallen into the water. Curious, he picked it up, and to his amazement, it transformed into a lemon in his hands.

He took the lemon home to his wife, who placed it in a vessel filled with rice. The next day, a miracle occurred, and they discovered a beautiful baby girl in place of the lemon. The childless couple was overjoyed and named her Suvarna Kedage. The neighbours speculated how could they have a baby girl when the brahmanatti (brahmin's wife) did not show any signs of pregnancy.

As time passed, Suvarna Kedage grew up fast; in a day, she looked like she aged a month, and in a month, she appeared to be of a year. Soon, she attained puberty before marriage. But in those days, if a girl reached puberty before marriage, she had to be abandoned in the forest. With a heavy heart, Suvarna Kedage was left all alone in the forest of Sankarmale, blindfolded and crying for help.

A toddy tapper by the name of Sayana Baidya, on his usual routine, was going up a tree. The tree broke and fell down, just missing the girl by a few inches.

'Who is it that draws toddy from the tree?' she asked, 'If you untie the cloth then you are my brother and I shall be indebted as your sister.'

'How can I untie the cloth as you are a brahmanatti and I am a mere Billava by caste?' Upon hearing her faint cries, he said, 'All right, let me go and seek permission from my master.'

Thus, Sayana Baidya went all the way to his master, Parmale Ballal, 'I found a brahmin girl in Sankarmane forest who requested me to untie her blindfold. What should I do?'

'You had a sister called Deyi who died a few years ago. Think that God has sent her back to you. I think you should do as she says, and then bring her with you and take care of her as your sister,' the master spoke thus.

This way, Sayana Baidya rushed back and helped the poor girl. He rescued her and brought her home, renaming her Deyi Baidyadi. Later, he got her married to Kantanna Baidya. She had a daughter called Kinnidaaru* who was married off at the age of seven. Deyi Baidyadi lived a happy life with her husband, away from the horrors of the forest. The people of the village marvelled at the wonder of her rescue, and she came to be known as very proficient in folk medicine.

In some versions, Kinnidaaru is the daughter of Sayana baidya's deceased sister, Deyi (after whom Suvarna Kedage was named Deyi).

Chapter 2 — Ballal's Dream

In the midst of his slumber, Parmale (Padmale/Parumale) Ballal is visited by a dream fraught with ominous signs. Alarmed by their implications, he seeks the counsel of an astrologer, who interprets the omens as forewarnings of impending calamities. The dream portends the ravaging of crops by wild beasts, the prevalence of unrighteousness within the kingdom, and the desolation of the neglected shrine of Naagabrahma.

To address the problem of the wild animals, the Ballal with the people of his kingdom, ventured into the jungle on a hunting expedition. But as he was taking aim, a poisonous thorn pierced the sole of his foot. His people tie up logs together and prepare a stretcher to carry him to his manor house. He instructs his ministers to find an expert in folk medicine who could treat him.

Many treatments later, he found no improvement in his condition. It was only getting worse. There were rumours that the Parmale Ballal may not survive much longer.

'I may die soon if I am not cured. Who in this land or beyond could give me medicine?' Parmale inquired from his servants.

One of the servants replied, 'Such wounds could only be healed by Sayana Baidya, but he cannot see due to old age. There is a woman, the wife of Kantanna Baidya, and sister of Sayana Baidya. Her name is Deyi Baidyadi. She is very good with folk medicine.'

'Bring her at once to my court!'

Chapter 3 — The Birth of the Twins

Deyi Baidyadi was pregnant when she received an urgent message from the powerful and wealthy Parmale Ballal. Without a moment's hesitation, she set out on a journey to save the Parmale's life. Though Parmale sent a palanquin for her, Deyi placed the medicines in it. She chose to walk with her husband Kantanna and brother Sayana to his manor house.

Despite the custom that forbade people of her community from stepping inside a manor house, Deyi boldly broke the tradition and diagnosed Parmale Ballal's ailment. This did not go well with Ballal's minister, Budhyanta and his colleagues. Nevertheless, Deyi Beidyadi used her vast knowledge of herbs and incantations to cure him, and within a few days, Parmale was able to walk once again.

In gratitude for saving his life, Parmale Ballal showered Deyi with gifts. He vowed to give a share of his kambala field to her children and made a promise of gifts whenever they demanded. But just as she was about to leave for home, Deyi was suddenly overcome with labour pain. Parmale Ballal provided a shelter for the pregnant woman in a shed of his manor house, where she gave birth to twins.

On the sixteenth day after the birth of her children, Deyi went to a nearby brook to wash her soiled clothes. It was there that tragedy struck*. Without warning, a coconut fell from a palm tree and landed on her head, killing her instantly.

As the news of her tragic demise spread far and wide, people mourned the loss of the gifted healer who had touched so many lives. Parmale Ballal was heartbroken at her passing and vowed to look after the twins, in honour of the brave young woman who had given her life for him. The proud Parmale Ballal named the first-born Koti, after the cornerstone of the temple at Koteshvar, and the second one Chennaya, after the cornerstone of the temple at Chatteshvar. Parmalle Ballal entrusted their care to Sayana Baidya.

Alternate accounts suggest that she met her untimely end through poisoning, orchestrated by Budhyanta and his cohorts as part of a nefarious conspiracy.

Chapter 4 — The Twins and Budhyanta

A few years passed. The twins grew into fine young children.

'O uncle Sayana, we wish to play with other children,' the twins said one day.

'My children, you are very young. Other children your age are only learning to crawl and speak,' Sayana said.

'You think of us as ordinary children, uncle! If you don't let us play, then we shall go on our own.'

'No, I cannot allow you to play,' he said strictly.

The boys began crying. Sayana's wife came and inquired why they were crying.

'If we had a mother or father, then they would have allowed us to play,' the twins complained.

So, the aunt called Sayana and told him about the twins's demand. Sayana summoned the twins and sat them on the swinging cot and said, 'Okay, you can go and play.'

Thus, the twins went on to play with grown-up children that also included Budhyanta's sons. They were not keen on having them join in. Despite the reluctance of the other children, Koti and Chennaya participated and triumphed in all the games. But the defeated children, unable to bear their loss, went to their father, Budhyanta, the minister in Ballal's court.

The minister, who had already harboured resentment towards the twins' mother for breaking tradition and entering Ballal's manor, scolded Koti and Chennaya for their victory. He went on to take their ball and berries.

'Go ahead, Budhyanta. Keep our belongings in your attic. But remember,' the twins challenged the minister and prophesized, 'one day we will enter your house to get them back.'

As already mentioned, the people of their caste were not allowed inside the house of the minister. So, from that day onwards, Budhyanta's grudge intensified against them and he secretly plotted their downfall, waiting for the perfect opportunity to strike.

Chapter 5 — Kambala

In their adolescent years, Koti and Chennaya embarked upon a journey to learn the art of fighting at a garadi, with the approval of their caretaker uncle, Sayana. After rigorous training, they became skilled warriors and were well-known for their prowess in combat.

Parmalle Ballal, impressed by their achievements, awarded them the promised lower division of a kambula field, while Budhyanta, who was envious of their success, was granted the upper division. This only fueled Budhyanta's resentment towards the twins as farming and landholding was not reserved for people of the twins' caste.

One day, while Budhyanta was on his way to an astrologer to find a favorable time to perform Kambala, which was a traditional buffalo race in the field that will initiate the process of sowing the seeds, he had to pass in front of the twins's house. Upon seeing him, they intercepted him and inquired about his purpose.

'I am consulting the astrologer to find the most auspicious time for Kambala,' Budhyanta replied.

'In that case, would you be kind enough to ask the astrologer to give us the same information?' Koti and Chennaya requested.

Budhyanta agreed. Upon meeting with the astrologer, he gave the same dates for both parties to sow the seeds. Budhyanta wanted to be the first to sow the seeds, so he lied and told the twins that they should hold Kambala the next Tuesday, even though it was a New Moon Day, and no farming activity was to take place on such a day.

The twins suspected that Budhyanta was lying and held their sowing ceremony on the same day as him. To ease the burden on the village, they declared that those with two pairs of oxen could send one pair to their field and the other to Budhyanta's. Those with only one pair could choose which field to send them to.

Despite Budhyanta's attempt to sabotage them, the twins finished their work before him and even sent their oxen to help him complete his task on time. However, Budhyanta felt humiliated and took out his anger on the men and oxen that were sent to his field by the twins.

On the seventh day of sowing, Koti tended to his fields, while Chennaya journeyed deep into the Sankarmane forest to gather toddy. As Koti approached his field, he was met with a most heinous sight: Budhyanta, the corrupt minister, had maliciously released water from his own field to destroy the crops of Koti and Chennaya. When Koti confronted Budhyanta about his treachery, the fiend hurled vile insults at him, inciting the twins' wrath.

Determined to deliver justice, Koti and Chennaya pursued the wicked minister with swords in hand. On that fateful day, the sun was hot and the winds were dry. As fate would have it, the evil Budhyanta met his demise at the hands of the heroic twins, Koti and Chennaya. They dug a deep pit with a spade and buried Budhyanta's lifeless body, adorning the tool with his clothes and ornaments before placing it on his seat as a grim reminder of his crimes.

But the twins' quest for vengeance did not end there. They had to keep the word that they had given during their childhood.

They sought out Budhyanta's wife, who was taken aback by their presence, as she knew of the rivalry between them and her husband. The twins spun a yarn of how Budhyanta had grown weary from toiling in the sun all day and required some refreshments. The unsuspecting wife obliged, inviting them into her home for a meal. The twins revealed that they had only consumed two meals that day, having already feasted on their fill. The wife then asked if they desired anything else, to which Koti and Chennaya responded by informing her that long ago, Budhyanta had seized some of their belongings by force and stowed them away in his attic. Moved by their plight, the wife retrieved the items—a ball and some berries—and returned them to their rightful owners.

As the wife made her way to the field, her eyes beheld a gruesome sight—her husband's garb was askew upon a tool. In that moment, she knew with a heavy heart that the twins had brought her beloved to his untimely end. The widow cursed the twins for snatching marital bliss away from her.

Chapter 6—Promise to the Mother

News of the minister's death spread like wildfire throughout the kingdom, reaching the ears of the great Parmale Ballal. The twins were summoned at the court. Ballal presided over his court, his regal demeanor commanding respect. As Koti-Chennaya entered, they bowed. However, Ballal's countenance darkened as he addressed them sternly, admonishing their actions. 'You have transgressed boundaries that should never have been crossed! Prepare to face the consequences.'

'Sir, before we proceed with the hearing, we want you to remember the promise you made to our mother before she died.'

'Let us not conflate your misdeeds with entitlements,' Ballal retorted.

'Agreed, punish us for our crime, but honour what is rightfully ours!' Koti implored.

'Else, who will receive these gifts when we are no more?' Chennaya interjected.

Ballal, reluctantly, inquired, 'What do you seek?'

Without hesitation, Koti made his demands. 'A vast field to the north of the manor house, where we could sow our crops and live peacefully.'

Ballal hesitated. 'That is not feasible.'

'Then, a milch buffalo that never runs dry!' Koti persisted.

'I require it,' Ballal replied curtly.

Undeterred, Koti pressed on. 'And the jackfruit tree that bears fruit year-round!'

Ballal waved off the request. 'Move on, ask for something else ...'

'Then grant us the gardens of your wives!'

But the king, now gnashing his teeth with rage, said, 'How dare you?'

'What about your royal sword, why don't you gift us that?' Koti challenged, his resolve unyielding.

Ballal's rage flared. 'You, who were nurtured within our walls, dare to demand the gardens of my wives and even the royal sword itself! Such insolence cannot be tolerated.' He motioned to his attendants, ordering Koti-Chennaya's arrest.

However, no one dared to lay a hand on them. The twins receded and declared, 'you have six months to fulfill our demand.' After that the twins decided to leave for Panja*.

In some versions, Parmale Ballal repents the decision and starts missing the twins who had grown up in his kingdom.

Once Koti and Chennaya encountered an elderly Brahmin along their path. Curious about their background, the Brahmin inquired about their caste. Koti responded proudly, 'We are of the Billava caste,' while Chennaya added with conviction, 'And Brahmins by our actions.'

The Brahmin offered water from a pot.

Chennaya retorted confidently, 'No, we shall not drink water from this pot. I shall extend my sword. Pour water on the opposite side, and we shall quench our thirst.'

Thus, with steady hands, they drank from the blade without spilling a single drop. The Brahmin stood in awe, astonished by the remarkable feat. He recognized the extraordinary nature of the duo before him. Revealing himself to be a fortune-teller, the old man prophesied a challenging journey ahead for Koti and Chennaya, but assured them that their names would be remembered for eternity. The twins then continued their journey.

Chapter 7 — A Reunion

During their arduous journey through Panja, the twin brothers found themselves plagued by an insistent thirst. Weary, they halted their footsteps before a humble abode, beckoning its inhabitant for assistance. With raised voices, they called out, 'Hello? Is anyone home?'

A woman named Kinnidaaru responded from within, her voice carrying through the narrow passage. 'Who seeks entry?' she inquired. 'If you are a Bunt or a landlord, find shelter beneath the padmakatte coconut tree. If you are a Shetty or a Brahmin, rest beneath the shade of the betel-leaf creepers. But if you share the same caste and clan as I, come and be seated on the swing inside.'

Following her instructions, both brothers settled themselves under the padmakatte, seeking respite from their thirst. They beseeched Kinnidaaru to provide them with a tumbler of water.

Standing on the threshold, Kinnidaaru spoke with caution, 'There are no male members present at the moment, so I will not step beyond the threshold.'

She extended a silver goblet filled with water, but the brothers hesitated. 'We shall not partake of this water without proper introduction,' they insisted. 'Before quenching our thirst, we must know your caste and status. Share your identity with us, and then we shall drink.'

Curiosity piqued, Kinnidaaru revealed her caste and clan identity. 'My mother is Deyi Baidedi, my father Kantanna, and my uncle Sayana. I am their first daughter, Kinnidaaru. Since my marriage at the age of seven, I have resided far away, and it is through hearsay that I learn of my mother giving birth to twin sons in my absence. They are named Koti and Chennaya, handsome and strong beyond compare. Alas! I have not laid eyes on them or heard their voices. I long to embrace them, to have a conversation with them, and to feel their weight upon my shoulders. Did you not inquire about our caste and tradition?'

As Kinnidaaru* narrated her tale, Koti and Chennaya exchanged astonished glances. Suddenly, they leaped to their feet and exclaimed, 'Ah, sister! We are none other than Koti and Chennaya, your brothers!' Kinnidaaru's joy knew no bounds. She stood there, speechless, overwhelmed by the enormity of the moment. She scrutinized her long-lost siblings from head to toe, holding their hands tightly, singing with sheer elation. She wondered which one was the elder and which the younger. In a jubilant frenzy, she led them into the chambers within, gently swaying them in a swing chair. She served water in goblets and milk in plates to her younger siblings.

*In some versions, Kinnidaaru is mentioned as the daughter of the original sister of Sayana Baidya who had passed away before Suvarna Kedage was found.

Meanwhile, Kinnidaaru's husband, Payya Baidya, returned home from his work tapping palm toddy. As he entered the house, he noticed the unfamiliar faces and exclaimed, 'Who are these cruel rogues who have arrived in our midst, carrying the weight of a human killing?'

Fearful and alarmed, Payya Baidya quickly lodged his curved sickle on the wooden rooftop, attempting to flee through the small door. Observing their brother-in-law's desperate struggle, Koti and Chennaya stepped forward, repeatedly addressing him as their brother-in-law. However, Payya felt caught between the towering figures, suffocating in their presence.

With utmost haste, Kinnidaaru revealed that Koti and Chennaya were her long-lost brothers. Payya Baidya, relieved and overjoyed, extended a warm welcome to the twins, embracing them as part of their humble household. The brothers found solace in the comfort of their newfound family, residing there for several days. The twins helped in various matters of the region and people started singing their glories.

The ruler of Panja, Kemara Ballal, came to know of them and wanted to meet them. However, his close aide, Chandugidi, disliked Payya Baidya. So, he poisoned Kemara's mind by reminding him of the way the twins had left Parmale Ballal fuming.

Meanwhile, the twins stated their desire to meet Kemara Ballal. So, Payya Baidya escorted them to meet the ruler of Panja. Unbeknownst to the twins and Payya, Chandugidi had already received a notification from Parmale Ballal to capture the twins and had issued an arrest warrant. Deceptively disguising his intentions, Chandugidi devised a plan to apprehend them while feigning a warm reception. Little did the twins realize the perils that awaited them in the court of Kemara Ballal.

Chapter 8 — The Trap

And so, it came to be that Koti and Chennaya were imprisoned in a foul dungeon*, where poisonous scorpions scuttled and bats hung ominously overhead. Yet, the twins were not to be defeated so easily. With unyielding faith in Bermeru, they beseeched the deity with all their might. In a miraculous turn of events, a slender crack appeared in the dungeon wall, and a beam of light shone through it. The twins mustered all their strength and kicked the wall with all their might until it finally gave way, granting them their freedom from the dank and oppressive prison.

Under the cover of darkness, as they walked the path, a few soldiers laid eyes upon the twins. Taken in custody, they were brought to the court of Devanna Ballal of Enmuru. It was there that the twins came to know of the ongoing border dispute between Devanna and Kemara Ballal. Devanna saw an opportunity in the heroic twins, offering them shelter and protection in exchange for their allegiance in the impending battle. The twins, too, needed refuge and accepted the offer, forging a marriage of convenience.

In some versions, it is mentioned that Chandugidi ordered the twins to build a palatial structure overnight. This structure, called Dindumale, was made to trap the brothers.

However, when Kemara Ballal learned of this development, he was filled with deep concern. He waited for a chance to strike, and it presented itself in the form of a wild boar hunt. Koti and Chennaya joined others in the hunt, chasing the boar into Panja, Kemara's territory. The animal met its end in Panja, and the twins carried it with them back to Enmuru. Kemara Ballal seized the opportunity and wrote a letter of complaint to Devanna, demanding the return of the boar or else face a battle.

Undeterred, the twins informed Devanna that they were ready to take on Kemara Ballal's army. Ballal of Enmuru gave the clarion call for battle gauging the despicable intentions of Kemara Ballal and his troops. They prepared their own forces and marched off to war.

Chapter 9 — The Final War

In the midst of an atmosphere pregnant with impending tragedy, the courageous duo of Koti and Chennaya sought to secure the future of their ancestral lands before setting foot upon the treacherous path of war. Kujumba Kaanja, their nephew and trusted guardian of their fertile agricultural expanse, stood before them as they entrusted him with a solemn charge. Their voices quivered with determination and a touch of melancholy as they conveyed their wishes, 'If our triumphant return graces this land, its inheritance shall be ours. But if cruel fate decrees otherwise, it falls upon you, Kujumba Kaanja, to safeguard and cultivate the bountiful soil of Ekanadka.'

With heavy hearts and a lingering sense of foreboding, the gallant brothers embarked on their fateful journey. The plains of Panja, a battleground shrouded in darkness and turmoil, beckoned them to embrace their destinies. Side by side, they stood upon that hallowed ground, their gazes locked in a solemn exchange.

Koti, the elder sibling, spoke with a mix of vulnerability and resolve, 'Oh, my beloved younger brother, how shall we discern if the merciless hand of fate claims one of us amidst the chaos of battle?'

'Should my earthly existence come to a tragic end, I shall metamorphose into a mournful crow perched upon the stone lip of the cavern's well. You must keep a watchful eye upon it. And if, by cruel happenstance, it is you who breathes your last, you must manifest in that very same form!'

In the face of imminent peril, Koti issued a command to Chennaya, his voice brimming with fraternal love and a tinge of desperation, 'When shall our spirits reunite, dear brother? Where and when shall we find solace in each other's presence once more?' These words, laden with the weight of impending separation, pierced the air, resounding with tragic undertones. With a heavy embrace and tear-stained farewells, the brothers parted ways, their souls burdened by the cruel dance of destiny.

Clad in their battle-worn armour, Koti ascended to the higher plateau of the treacherous battleground, where the forces clashed with unyielding ferocity. Meanwhile, Chennaya positioned himself in the lower region, ready to face whatever horrors awaited him. The stage was set for a heart-wrenching tale of sacrifice and impending doom. The final act, cloaked in darkness and tragedy, was about to unfold.

Chennaya showcased his valour, swiftly dispatching any who dared to obstruct him with a swift swing of his dagger. Armed with bow and arrow, he drove off any soldier who dared to challenge him. He killed Chandugidi as well.

Simultaneously, Koti fought valiantly on the higher plateaus, relentlessly pursuing his adversaries, and scattering those who stood in his path. Those who found themselves engaged in combat with Koti at the same level were met with the piercing edge of his dagger. Panja suffered heavy blows at the hands of these heroic warriors.

In a climactic twist of fate, the battlefield quivered with anticipation as Parmale Ballal himself, a figure of authority that had raised the warrior twins and then vanquished them from his kingdom, emerged onto the scene. A resolute leader at the helm of an imposing force, he brazenly announced his alliance with the Panja unit, boldly declaring his intention to engage the indomitable forces of Koti and Chennaya in a battle for supremacy. The clash that ensued, a clash of titans, unfolded over the passage of seven twilight-laden dusks and eight dawn-kissed mornings, as the warriors grappled for dominance amidst a swirling tempest of valour and bloodshed. Yet, in the face of unparalleled courage and unwavering resolve, victory remained elusive, slipping through the fingers of those who dared challenge the might of these twin heroes. Witnessing his own destruction unfold on the battlefield, Parmale Ballal schemed a treacherous ploy against his opponents.

While Koti, the embodiment of strength, was engrossed in the fray, a sinister arrow, guided by malice, found its mark, plunging into his chest with unforgiving precision. Bewildered and wounded, Koti turned to confront his assailant, his eyes locking with the chilling gaze of Parmale Ballal, a man armed with a bow curved like the twisted tendrils of treachery itself.

'Oh, Ballal!' Koti's voice, tinged with a mix of disbelief and agony, reverberated through the battlefield. 'How could you, after nurturing us with care, raising us from the depths of despair following our mother's departure? How could you, a guardian turned betrayer, unleash your arrow upon my chest, targeting me from the shadows like a craven assassin? How could you?'

Images of their shared past, of tender moments and intertwined destinies, flickered before Parmale Ballal's eyes. The weight of remorse bore down upon his conscience, rendering him speechless, his head bowed in shame. Koti, wounded and weary, turned away from the despicable scene, beckoning the Ballals of Panja and

Enmuru to gather at his side. 'Henceforth, all three Ballals must live together in harmony,' he declared, expressing his final desire.

With a heavy heart and a lingering gaze cast upon the assembled kings, Koti drew his last breath, surrendering his mortal frame to the embrace of everlasting peace. Thus, Koti Baidya bid farewell to the physical realm, his spirit merging with the ethereal realm. A descent into the hallowed precincts of Lord Bermer beckoned, a quest for reunion at the divine's right side. Yet, before he could cross the threshold into the realm of the divine, a celestial voice resounded, echoing through the sacred space. It said, 'Do not descend into this yard, do not touch this wall. Why have you arrived alone? Both of you were born together, raised together. Return at once! Escort your brother as well. You siblings are eternally united, destined to be so!'

In the sombre realm of the battlefield, Chennaya, having emerged triumphant, embarked on a desperate quest to find his elder brother, his heart filled with hope and trepidation. Yet, alas! His search proved futile, for his beloved sibling was nowhere to be found. It was then, upon the desolate mouthstone of the well, nestled within the cavern's depths, that he beheld a sight that shattered his soul—a solitary crow, perched in mournful solitude.

'Oh, brother! Have you forsaken me to endure this desolation alone? Is there anything left for me in this world but a void of emptiness?' Overwhelmed by an ocean of sorrow, Chennaya's anguished cry reverberated through the forlorn expanse. And in a desperate act born of inconsolable grief, he hurled his head against the very mouthstone, his skull colliding with a resounding thud.

Thus, in a tragic tableau of suffering, Chennaya relinquished his mortal existence, his body collapsing upon the lifeless form of his cherished brother. Writhing in torment, he surrendered his earthly essence, transcending into the ethereal realm, and joined his brother as radiant spirits destined to roam the celestial planes. While the flickering flames of their mortal vessels succumbed to darkness, these immortal siblings emerged as an everlasting and luminescent beacon adorning the sacred realm of the spirits.

Haunted by the guilt of slaying Koti and Chennaya with their own hands, the remorseful Ballals sought redemption. As an act of expiation, they erected garadi worship centres across their lands. The legend of Koti Chennaya would forever be etched upon the annals of Tulu Nadu's rich folklore.

Notes

The Revolutionary Hero

The revolutionary hero or the rebel hero is an archetype that usually hails from a lower social stratum or an oppressed community, utilizing their wit, might and bravery to vanquish their oppressors and usher in a more egalitarian society. In Tulu lore, the valiant brothers Koti and Chennaya are deified and hailed as 'baidyarlu' or 'beiderlu'. Their tale of torment and rebellion serves as an embodiment of heroic glory for the regional populace. The beiderlu, much like the revolutionary heroes of literature and global mythology, embody a protagonist who dares to challenge the norm and fight against oppression and injustice.

The birth of Koti and Chennaya into the Billava caste was a significant event. The Billava, an ethnic group of the region, were engaged in tasks such as toddy tapping and small-scale farming in the olden times. Many in the community carried the suffix 'Baidya' or 'Poojary' added to their names. Baidya signifies a physician, and the female is often referred to as Baidyadi, as in the story you just read. On the other hand, Poojary denotes performers of pooja or worship in Daivaaradhane and kola ceremonies.

The term 'Billava' is believed to originate from 'billu' or the traditional bow and arrow, owing to their mastery in wielding the billu. For this reason, some scholars believe that they may have been bowmen and original inhabitants of the region. Although today caste discrimination is punishable, there was a time when the members of the community were not allowed inside a temple of worship (Sturrock, 1894, pg, no. 172). In the folktale, Koti-Chennaya were no exception to the caste-based discrimination that was prevalent in society at their time. Despite their proximity to power centres, the heroic twins were subjected to constant treachery and harassment. Scholars have estimated that Koti and Chennaya may have lived in the seventeenth or eighteenth century, a time when the rigid caste system dominated Indian society.

Garadi

Unlike the daivas, the beiderlu are worshipped in a 'garadi'—a gymnasium or arena where combatants were originally trained in martial arts. Once akin to the 'kalari' of Kerala, these traditional training grounds now serve as a memorial or a sacred precinct dedicated to the beiderlu in Tulu Nadu. Though the heroic twins enjoy an exalted status as icons of veneration, they remain quite distinct from the daivas, as discernible in the dance ritual.

5

Pilichandi

PILICHANDI OR PILICHAMUNDI IS A SPIRIT DEITY that is associated with tigers or leopards. The name 'pili' means a 'big cat' in Tulu, and it reflects the fear and respect that people had for these animals. In some parts, Pilichandi is also known as Vyaaghra Chamundi (vyaaghra means tiger). The worship of Pilichandi may have originated from the need to appease the spirit that controlled the big cats, that is, tigers or leopards, and to prevent them from attacking the villages or the cattle. This is like the scholarly theory of how people may have started worshipping the spirit of the boar, to protect their crops from being destroyed by wild boars. Thus, Pilichandi is a protective spirit just like Panjurli.

Chapter 1 — In the Beginning ...

In the beginning, when the universe was young and the waters of the primordial ocean stretched to the horizon, a mighty ball of fire rose from the depths and lit up the sky—the glorious sun. On its flanks, two birds nestled, a male and a female. They were splendid creatures, with feathers of dazzling colours and songs of sweet melody.

One day, as they soared in the air, they caught the eye of Parvati. She was enchanted by their grace and charm, and invited them to her abode in Kailasa. There, Parvati showered them with affection and gifts, and made them her companions.

As the seasons changed, the birds grew older and wiser, and Ishvara, Parvati's husband, fashioned many marvels on the earth below. He separated the infinite waters of the primordial ocean into seven seas, and filled them with fish and pearls. He raised mountains and valleys, and planted trees and flowers.

Chapter 2—The Egg

One day, the female bird felt a stirring in her womb, and knew that she was with child. She longed for a rare pollen that grew only on a distant island, beyond the seventh sea. Her loyal husband vowed to fetch it for her, no matter the cost. He kissed her goodbye and flew away, across the vast waters. But as he reached his destination, night fell, and a storm raged. The wind howled and the rain poured. The flowers that bore the pollen closed their petals, hiding their treasure. The male bird searched frantically for an open blossom, but found none. He spotted one that seemed to glow faintly in the dark, and dove towards it. But it was a trap—a carnivorous plant that snapped its jaws around him. He struggled to free himself, but it was too late. He was trapped inside the flower.

Back at Kailasa, Parvati and Ishvara came to visit their feathered friend. They found her in tears, pining for her husband. She told them of his quest for the pollen, and how he had not returned. She prayed to Ishvara for his safety, offering her first-born egg as a sacrifice. Ishvara heard her plea, and moved by her devotion, he granted her wish. He commanded the flower to release its captive, and let him fly back home.

But destiny had a strange surprise in store for the couple. When the female bird laid her egg, it rolled down from its nest and cracked open before its time. From within emerged a tiny tiger cub, with stripes of black and gold. Parvati was delighted by this wonder, and took the cub under her care. She assigned him the sacred duty of watching over her cows, the gentle creatures that grazed on the slopes of Kailasa. But Parvati and Ishvara soon noticed that their cows were vanishing one by one from their fields.

Chapter 3 — The Cattle and the Tiger

Parvati was deeply troubled by the loss of her cows. They were her pride and joy, and she loved them dearly. She could not bear to see them disappear one by one, without a trace. She begged Ishvara to find out who was behind this mystery, and to bring them to justice. Ishvara agreed to help his beloved wife. He decided to disguise himself as a cow, and join the herd that grazed on the green pastures of Kailasa. He hoped to catch the culprit red-handed, and to put an end to the carnage.

Thus, metamorphosing into a cow, he slipped into the crowd of cattle, and followed them as they wandered around the hills. He kept a watchful eye on his surroundings, looking for any signs of danger. He noticed a small figure on a nearby gooseberry (amla/nellikai) tree, nibbling on the ripe fruits. It was the cub, who had grown up under Parvati's care. He looked happy and content, unaware of Ishvara's presence. The cub finished his meal, and jumped down from the tree. He walked towards a lake, where he quenched his thirst with the clear water. He licked his lips, and said to himself, 'This water tastes so sweet, I am sure that the cows who drink the water from the lake all the time must be tasting sweeter.' He eyed a cow that was bending down to drink from the lake. He crouched low, and prepared to pounce. But he had chosen the wrong target. The cow was none other than Ishvara himself, who had seen his every move. As soon as the tiger leaped in the air, Ishvara revealed his true form. He was a towering figure, with four arms and three eyes. He caught the tiger in mid-air, and held him firmly in his grip. 'O Pili (tiger),' he thundered, 'we entrusted you to take care of the cows and instead you were killing them. Go, now! I banish you from Kailasa.'

Ishvara, enraged by the cub's betrayal, changed it into a spirit called Pilichandi, who had a fearsome appearance and a terrible roar. Ishvara cast him out of Kailasa, and sent him to Earth. There, he would have to watch over the animals and crops, and protect the devotees. It would never see Parvati or Kailasa again. But Parvati, who had a soft spot for the cub, felt sorry for it. She took pity on its fate, and made a promise. She said, 'O Pilichandi, do not despair. One day, I will come down to Earth as a goddess, and I will choose you as my vaahana (vehicle). You will be my loyal companion, and I will shower you with my blessings.' Pilichandi was touched by Parvati's kindness. It bowed its head, and thanked her for her mercy. Thus, Pilichandi descended to Tulu Nadu.

Notes

Variations in the Folktale

The story that you just read is one of the many versions of how Pilichandi came into being. It is based on a mythological tale that involves Parvati, Shiva, and a pair of birds. Interestingly, some variations of the epic of Koti-Chennaya also begin with the same birds. There is also a version in which the protective God is Surya

Narayana (sun) instead of Ishvara (Shiva). When the female bird prays to Surya, he appears before her, and because of the sudden appearance of the sun in the sky, the lotus (in which the male bird was trapped) blooms, and the bird escapes death.

As I mentioned, oral traditions vary depending on the region or the religious beliefs of the storytellers. For example, in another version, there is no mention of gooseberries. Instead, the tiger sees blood dripping from a cow's wound, and mistakes it for berry juice. It then kills the cow to drink its blood. I have also heard of a version in which the female bird offers the egg to Shiva who is in Naagaloka attending some ceremony. Shiva takes the egg home and places it safely until it hatches. However, due to some mischief, the egg cracks and out comes the resplendent tiger. The story shows the rich and diverse oral tradition of the region, and the creative imagination of the people who narrated it. It also reflects the cultural and ecological aspects of their lives, such as their relationship with nature, animals and gods.

There is an intriguing folk tale originating from North Kerala, which recounts the story of Shiva and Parvati incarnating as tigers and giving birth to six tiger cubs in Tulurvanam, Paanathur. One day, while playing in the jungle, the hungry tiger cubs wandered into a prominent man named Kurumbrathiri's cattle shed and devoured all the cows before retreating into the forest.

Enraged by the loss of his cattle, Kurumbrathiri ordered a hunter to track down and capture the culprit cubs. However, the hunter met his demise at the claws of the fierce tiger cubs. Concerned by the hunter's absence, Kurumbrathiri set out to search for him. However, when his servants attempted to lift his palanquin, it remained stationary. Sensing the supernatural involvement of the tiger cubs, Kurumbrathiri realised their divine nature and decided to venerate the tiger spirits in the region (Unnikrishnan, 2023, pg. no. 152)

From Burnell's Pages

Burnell gives an intriguing account of Pilichamundi in one of his manuscripts. It tells of a farmer named Manju Punja, who had been blessed with a piece of land in Tulu Nadu, on which he cultivated his crops with great care and dedication. However, despite his hard work, thieves began to ravage his land and stole everything from tender coconuts to paddy in the paddy fields. Distressed by these happenings, Manju Punja decided that he had to take matters into his own hands.

'I cannot let these arrogant rascals ruin everything,' he declared to his sister. 'I must teach them a lesson.'

Determined to summon a powerful spirit to aid him, Manju Punja packed his food, tied a turban on his head and donned his best attire. He made his way to the abode of Baloli, seeking a bhuta that could help him catch the thieves and put them to death.

Upon arriving, Baloli inquired about Manju Punja's purpose. 'In my farm, I had sown so many seeds and plants that grew to become great coconut palms and luscious paddy fields. But alas! Some rascals broke in and stole everything dear to me. I, therefore, came to you seeking a bhuta that can put the thieves to death,' Manju Punja cried.

Baloli asked, 'But what bhuta shall I give to you?'

'Give me a fearsome one that you worship, that Pilichamundi who can catch these thieves and kill them,' he said, handing over some money. Seeing the money, Baloli forgot to give any warnings and immediately fetched a betel leaf, drew an exact figure of the pilichamundi bhuta, and handed it to Manju Punja, saying, 'Take this with you to your farm. Worship with all your heart, and it will come to your aid.'

Overjoyed with his newfound power, Manju Punja took the betel leaf and went home, worshipping it with all his heart and soul. Though the Pilichamundi successfully took care of the thieves, a new problem arose in the household. At the end of the sixth month, the spirit killed Manju Punja's eldest daughter, followed by Punja himself at the end of the twelfth month, and then a woman named Gange at the end of the eighteenth month. Fearing for their own lives, the other members of the household took the spirit to the foot of a tree and started worshipping it there. Eventually, they built a sthana for the deity, and the killings came to an end.

Burnell then goes on to mention how the spirit then travelled to other places, before finally settling in a sthaana at Mukkodivalakuda. Interestingly, the story of Manthradevathe is strikingly similar to this one as you will see in the next chapter.

6

Manthradevate

DEEP IN THE LUSH SOUTH-WESTERN COAST OF India, where the waves of the Arabian Sea lap gently against the sandy shores, there exists a land of enchanting stories and captivating deities. The tales of this land are not bound by the lines that demarcate the modern-day borders of the two states, as the folklore and deities of Tulu Nadu and Kerala are deeply intertwined and share a common bond.

Chapter 1—Not Merely a Stone

There is a fascinating story of divine intervention and the discovery of a powerful deity that stems from Kerala. It is said that a prominent Tantri (Thanthri) of Kerala once visited his kin in Southern Tulu Nadu. During his stay, he was privileged to witness their cousin perform the worship of the revered Varte at his home.

The sight left an indelible impression on the Tantri, and they yearned to have a similar divine presence in his own abode.

One day, as the Tantri was engrossed in his daily prayers, a miraculous event occurred that would forever change his life. A fiery limestone suddenly fell upon his clothes, and, considering it a rare and auspicious object, he placed it in a container made of stone. As the day wore on, the object cooled, and to his astonishment, a voice emanated from within the container.

'I am not merely a stone,' the voice proclaimed. 'I am a divine spirit, and I demand worship and offerings. Place me on the right side of your deity, and I will protect you and bestow great wealth upon you!'

The Tantri was thrilled and elated at this incredible turn of events. According to the instructions of this divine power, he named the deity 'Manthradevata' and worshiped it with the utmost devotion, recognizing it as a powerful protector and bestower of prosperity.

Chapter 2 — Kantu Baida's Dilemma

In Moodbidri lies the sacred ground of Iruvail, which boasts of the revered Durga Parameshwari temple. In this idyllic setting resided a man of modest means, Kantu Baida, who possessed a fertile land that bore the bounties of paddy and coconut palms. But as fate would have it, the incessant thievery of his crops left him in despair, a distress that mirrored that of Manju Punja in the fabled Pilichandi tale. Despite his valiant attempts to apprehend the robbers, the larceny continued unabated, and Kantu's family was wracked with anxiety.

It was during this time of woe that a friend of Kantu's paid him a visit. Upon seeing the crestfallen countenance of his comrade, he inquired, 'Pray tell, my friend, why do you wear the cloak of sorrow on your face?'

Kantu replied, 'Alas! I am at my wits' end. Thieves have ransacked my land, leaving me penniless and disheartened.'

His friend advised, 'Why don't we seek the counsel of the revered Tantri? He can bestow upon us a powerful deity who will safeguard your estate.'

And so, Kantu and his friend set out on a journey to the land of Kerala, where they arrived at the sanctum of the Tantri. Sitting in front of their ancestral deity, the Tantri inquired as to why Kantu had journeyed so far to seek their help. Kantu beseeched, 'Wise one, my life is in shambles. I implore you to grant me a potent deity that can protect my kin and my land.'

The Tantri responded, 'You may have any deity you desire. Would you like Varte? Maisandaya? Pilibhuta? A spirit with four or six arms? Tell me, which deity would you like?'

'I require a deity with a powerful kaarnika that can catch the thieves who are pilfering from me,' Kantu replied. His gaze was drawn to a vision that manifested next to the family deity. Pointing towards it, he said, 'I want that deity. Please send it with me.'

'Kantu, I urge you to choose any other deity but Manthradevathe,' the Tantri cautioned.

'Why not?' Kantu inquired.

'Because you are not ready to handle the immense power of our deity,' the Tantri warned.

But Kantu was adamant, 'I insist on having that deity.'

The Tantri pondered and finally declared, 'Very well, I will grant your request. But before I do, you must prove your worthiness.'

'How can I do that?' Kantu asked.

'You must travel the length and breadth of the land, learning a dozen different languages. Only then will you be considered worthy of receiving the deity,' the Tantri replied.

Kantu was crestfallen, for the task was daunting and near to impossible for a middle-aged man. However, as he departed from the

Tantri's abode, the divine power of Manthradevathe in her ethereal (spirit) form had also embarked on a mission to empower Kantu's quest. She entered his physical being and helped him travel to all the places and learn all the languages in a surprisingly short span of time. Thirty days later, Kantu returned to the Tantri's dwelling.

The Tantri was pleased to know that Kantu had fulfilled the task, and he was sure that Manthradevathe had blessed him. So, he handed him a piece of limestone, which symbolized the spirit of Manthradevathe, along with other offerings.

However, upon arriving home, Kantu, in his innocence, placed the precious limestone under a tree. That night, in his dreams, Manthradevathe appeared to him and spoke, 'O Kantu, I am pleased with your devotion, but hear me, I am not a daiva to be worshipped under a tree. I must be placed on a swinging cot inside a room. Then I will protect you, catch your thieves and fill your life with prosperity.'

Kantu, awoken by the divine command, immediately set about building a room for the deity and a swinging cot on which to place her. And so it was that Manthradevathe took her rightful place in the sanctum.

In time, Manthradevathe proved her worth as a protector and a harbinger of prosperity. She caught the thieves that plagued Kantu's village, and her kaarnika blazed like a beacon of divine justice. Her kaarnika (miracles) flashed not just in his house but also in the entire village. Kantu even received a boon from a Jain landlord—twelve acres of land. He accredited the change of his luck to the power of faith and the blessings of Manthradevathe.

Notes

Manthradevathe is a powerful female deity that is believed to come from Kerala. In the ritualistic dance of kola, the dancer representing

Mathradevathe, adorns himself with a black facial colour and wears a saree over his body. There is controversy regarding the offerings given to this deity as many believe that Manthradevathe accepts only sattvic food instead of meat. There is also strong connection between the deities of Tulu Nadu and their origins in Kerala. For example, some claim that Chamundi and Guliga have also arrived from beyond the ghats of Kerala. However, just like the origin stories of all other ancient daivas, the genesis of these stories has faded away with the passage of time.

7

The Story of Siri

THE SIRI PAADDANA, ONE OF THE GREATEST EPICS of Tulu Nadu, is the multi-generational tale of a Bant family, with its focal point being the remarkable figure of Siri. It is during the yearly Siri jaatre that the people of the region bear witness to the fascinating spectacle of thousands of women possessed by the Siri spirits. These spirits, distinct from the daivas, constitute an essential component of Tulu culture, and Siri's story explores the intricacies of the spirit world. It is to be noted here that Siris belong to Siri Loka, which is considered different from other lokas of Indian folklore and mythology.

Chapter 1—Ajjeru & Siri

Long ago, in the resplendent palace of Satyanaapura, resided a venerable gentleman, who was endearingly referred to as Berma Alva (Bermapalva/Bermanna) Ajjeru. He possessed numerous acres of arable land, the palace itself, and all the trappings of worldly wealth. But deep within his heart, he was besieged with sorrow, as he was deprived of the joy of progeny. He lost his mother and father at a young age. He had no spouse or children. His glory days were over and now he was wilting into old age. One day, while brooding over his unfortunate destiny, he summoned his trusted maid servant, Daaru.

'Pray tell me, what use is this mundane abundance I possess? Once I depart from this world, to whom shall I bequeath all that I have, no uncles above me nor nieces or grandchildren or siblings. I am childless,' he uttered with a heavy heart, gazing upon his loyal maid, Daaru.

Daaru replied in her gentle and reassuring voice, 'Fear not, O gracious master, for the benevolent Naaga Bermer will certainly show a way. '

Unconvinced by the answer, and determined to find solace, Bermu Ajjeru withdrew into the posh solitary recesses of his abode. 'I shall retire into the bollimaada and assume the life of retirement,' he instructed with tears welling up in his eyes. 'You shall oversee the affairs of the palace in my absence,' he directed his obedient maid servant.

Thus, Bermu Ajjeru sought refuge in the secluded silver chamber of his house, his heart heavy with grief and yearning. He slept on the earthen floor like a curled up baby. The tears that cascaded down his sorrowful eyes flowed out of his home and streamed to the feet of Naaga Bermer, beseeching his divine mercy.

Moved by the heartrending plight of the grieving old man, the magnanimous Naaga Bermer descended from the sacred realms of the spirits to the mortal plane to comfort him. Assuming the physical guise of a destitute brahmin, he set forth on his mission. As he reached the gateway of Ajjeru's palace, his guise elicited no more than a few crumbs of alms from Daaru, the diligent maid servant.

'Pray summon your master, for I shall not accept these morsels from your hands,' Bermer in the guise of brahmin asserted with resolute dignity.

Thus summoned, Bermu Ajjeru, with furrowed brow and sorrowful eyes, presented himself before the brahmin. With solicitous concern, the brahmin inquired, 'What ails you, O venerable sir, that you wear such a mournful visage?'

'I am bereft of an heir to inherit all that I possess,' lamented Ajjeru.

'Take heart, my dear sir, and embark upon the righteous path,' counselled the brahmin with sagacious intent. 'The shrines of your ancestors, which were long neglected, hold the key to your salvation. Rededicate them with piety and devotion, and your prayers shall be answered.'

With these words of solace, the brahmin turned and left, disappearing as mysteriously as he had appeared. And in his wake, Bermu Ajjeru felt a glimmer of hope rekindle within his despondent heart.

Brimming with newfound hope and faith, Ajjeru summoned his loyal servants and embarked on a sacred mission to honour his ancestors and appease the spirit deities. With due reverence, he conducted a ceremony of propitiation for his family's divine protector, the powerful Bermeru, and the other spirit deities.

Taking heed of the sagacious counsel of the brahmin, Ajjeru poured his resources into restoring the dilapidated shrines that had laid desolate for ages. He appointed a priest to perform daily rituals of worship and honour, and sought the wise counsel of an astrologer to fix an auspicious date for the annual festival of the shrines.

On the momentous day of the holy festival, the priest, with a soul filled with sanctity, offered Ajjeru a blessed prasaada—a vibrant pingaara (areca flower bunch), and a rich paste of aromatic sandalwood. Ajjeru, reverentially receiving the prasaada, held it close to his heart and after going home, placed it in a coffer for safekeeping.

As the night descended upon Satyanaapura palace, an ethereal glow emanated from the coffer in the inner sanctum. The dazzling beam of light, akin to a celestial aura, infused the chamber with a mystical energy that enraptured the very air.

At the break of dawn, as the soft hues of the sun brushed the sky with gentle strokes, Ajjeru stirred from his slumber, captivated by the distant echoes of a melodic cry that filled the room. Struck with bewilderment, he cautiously approached the coffer from where the sound originated. And lo! To his wonderment, he found, nestled in place of the areca flowers and sandalwood paste, a tender and radiant infant girl. Overcome with emotions, the old man, with trembling hands, took the baby into his loving arms and christened her 'Siri'.

With boundless joy and reverence, Bermu Ajjeru laid his cherished little one in a cozy cradle, where she slept peacefully, surrounded by the tranquil whispers of the divine forces that had graced her arrival. Being a creation of the spiritual world, Siri grew up at a miraculous speed.

In the tranquil fields of Kadengadi, Kanta Poonja was enjoying a leisurely stroll when he heard the lilting cries of a child wafting from the Satyanaapura palace. Immediately drawn to the sound, he made his way into the palace and chanced upon the child's grandfather, Bermu Ajjeru.

'Whose enchanting voice does utter such sweet cries?' inquired the curious Kantu Poonja.

'It is the voice of my child,' replied Ajjeru.

'Wondrous; I request you to show me this child,' Kantu Poonja beseeched.

Ajjeru was not initially keen to reveal Siri to the stranger, but after persistent entreaties, he reluctantly acquiesced and showed the little child to Kantu Poonja. Mesmerized by her beauty, Kantu Poonja tenderly placed a silk cloth in the cradle, a gesture symbolic of his proposal of marriage.

'When this girl comes of age, let her not be given to any other, nor be left to eat the leftovers of another's plate. Ajjeru, I am telling you; I will marry this girl when she comes of age, and no one else,' he fervently pleaded before departing.

In due course, Siri wed Kantu Poonja and they took up residence in Poonja's Balasuru Palace. Soon, the newly-wedded wife found herself with child, the harbinger of new life, bringing with it hope and joy. As the seventh month drew near, a significant ritual of 'bayake' was to be observed. Bayake was a joyous celebration, akin to a baby shower, among the community that hailed the arrival of the unborn infant and bestowed the mother-to-be with the blessings of motherhood. It was the mother-in-law who held this ceremony in the seventh month of pregnancy, at the husband's house. In olden times, the parents of the pregnant woman arrived at the auspicious event and then took their pregnant daughter to their home, where she would remain for the delivery and for the subsequent forty days. Bayake literally translates to 'desire', as the pregnant woman has the freedom to eat whatever her taste buds crave for. Thus, the day of bayake arrived for Siri.

Reluctantly, Kantu set out to buy his wife a saree and ornaments, that was needed for the ceremony. However, fate had other plans in store for Siri. While on her way back from the marketplace, Kantu made a halt at Siddu's residence, succumbing to temptation. Kantu became enmeshed in a web of debauchery, indulging in reckless squandering with Siddu, a woman of ill-repute. Siddu tried on the saree and ornaments meant for Siri, mocking the sanctity of the special occasion.

Upon discovering the truth, Siri's delicate sensibilities were deeply wounded. She refused to adorn herself with the garments that had been sullied by the touch of a prostitute, and instead chose to wear the clothes provided by her grandfather.

Chapter 2 — Kumara

In time, Siri gave birth to a healthy baby boy whom she named Kumara. However, her attempts to extend an invitation to her wayward husband and mother-in-law to come and visit their newborn were met with callous indifference. Thus, she cursed her husband and his family that everything that belonged to them should go barren.

Upon the birth of Kumara, Siri and Ajjeru sought the counsel of an astrologer, whose ominous countenance foretold of an impending danger.

Concerned, Siri inquired of him, 'What is it? Is everything well?'

The astrologer replied gravely, 'Ajjeru must not lay his eyes upon the child.'

Puzzled, Siri pressed, 'Why not?'

The astrologer intoned ominously, 'For Ajjeru shall die should he do so.'

Siri and Ajjeru heeded the astrologer's warning, and kept the infant away from Ajjeru's sight.

But fate had other plans. On one occasion, when Siri and Daaru were away by the river, the infant's cries drew Ajjeru to the cradle. Holding Kumara in his arms, he gazed at the child with joy and tenderness.

When Siri and Daaru returned, they discovered Ajjeru lying on the floor, struggling to save his last breath for Siri. As Siri cradled her dying grandfather's head on her lap, he whispered, 'The prophecy has come to pass. My time has come. Do not forsake your liberty, Siri, no matter what happens.'

Siri was left grief-stricken by Ajjeru's sudden demise. She reached out to her husband with news of her grandfather's passing to perform the funeral, but he did not respond. Resolute in her devotion, Siri set out to perform the last rites for her beloved grandfather.

In the wake of Bermu Ajjeru's death, a man by the name of Annu convened a village council to lay a claim on the Satyanaapura palace. Alas, the council, being inclined towards Annu, sided against Siri. But Siri, a determined and strong-willed woman, held her ground and put up a formidable fight. Despite her tenacity, the council eventually ordered her to relinquish the palace to Annu. With a heavy heart, Siri left the palace, but not before leaving a curse upon it. Her words echoed throughout the hallways as she swore that the palace would be reduced to ashes. She departed with her child, Kumara, and Daaru by her side. Mere moments after Siri and her family had left the premises, the once-grand palace was engulfed in a raging inferno, reducing it to nothing but smoldering ashes.

After the sudden and unexpected turn of events, Siri and Daaru went to Balasuru Palace, hoping to meet with Siri's husband, Kantu. But their visit took a sour turn when they were met with the cold and unwelcoming demeanor of Siri's mother-in-law.

'Pray tell, where is your son, my husband?' inquired Siri, her voice laced with concern.

'He is not home,' lied the mother-in-law in a dismissive tone, reluctant to entertain Siri and her little one.

'Where has he gone?' pressed Siri, determined to find her beloved husband.

'To Kaderi Karla, to pay taxes,' was the mother-in-law's curt response.

Siri's suspicions were aroused by this reply, and she dared to ask, 'Has he gone to pay taxes, or to meet his mistress, Siddu?'

Kantu, who had been inside the palace all that while, raged with fury. Those words from Siri's mouth seemed to have pierced Kantu's ears like arrows, as he appeared at the scene, shouting in a high-pitched voice, 'How is it that today in place of a rooster, a hen is heard crowing so loudly in my residence?'

With her eyes ablaze with fury, Siri clutched her precious Kumara closer to her chest and declared, 'I do not require your presence anymore. Henceforth, my newborn son, Kumara, shall be my guardian. I sever all ties with you, Kantu, and renounce you as my husband!'

Thus, Siri, with resolute determination, made the fateful decision to sever ties with Kantu and forsake the opulent halls of Balasuru Palace, never to return again. With her newborn son Kumara and faithful maid, Daaru, she set out on a journey fraught with danger and intrigue. Along the way, she encountered various individuals, both friend and foe, and used her mystical abilities to aid those in need and vanquish those who posed a threat. She bestowed blessings upon those who offered their assistance and cast dire curses upon those who dared to impede her progress.

As they traversed through the unfamiliar terrain, the trio eventually arrived at Bola, a tranquil haven of respite. While there, they attended to the needs of Kumara, and it was then that the miraculous happened. The baby boy suddenly let out a piercing cry, only to miraculously begin speaking.

'Oh, my dear mother,' spoke baby Kumara, his voice filled with prophecy, 'you shall not remain unwed for long, but alas, I shall not be present at your nuptials!'

'I mark your words, my son,' Siri replied.

'Now, if you can send me to the sacred realms of the spirit world, I shall be done,' he requested.

Without hesitation, Siri wielded her formidable powers, and with a flick of her wrist, the child vanished to the realm of maya. Daaru also requested to be sent with Kumara. Siri helped Daaru to vanish to maya as well.

Chapter 3 — Sonne & Gindye

In the heart of the jungle, where the leaves rustle and the birds sing, Siri's path was crossed by two valiant Kshatriya brothers, who were on a hunting expedition. Mesmerized by her resplendent beauty, they approached her with a proposal of marriage.

'Fair maiden, who among us two shall have the privilege of calling you his own?' the brothers asked with ardour.

With a serene smile, Siri replied, 'You are both akin to me as brothers, and it is not in my heart to favour one over the other.'

The brothers exchanged a meaningful glance and replied, 'Then we shall accept the honour of being your brothers, and henceforth, you shall be our dear sister. Please, allow us to escort you to our palace in a palanquin, where we may lavish you with the hospitality and respect befitting of your station.'

Thus, the Kshatriya brothers led Siri to their magnificent palace, where she was welcomed with open arms and treated with the utmost reverence. Amidst the grandeur of the palace, Kodsara Alva of Kottaradi manor arrived as a guest. The beguiling beauty of Siri caught his eye, and he was instantly smitten. Frequenting the palace, he finally proposed marriage to Siri, and she, the magical woman, agreed to be his wife, with her new brothers giving their assent. However, in the midst of this happiness, a storm brewed in the form of Kodsara Alva's first wife, Saamu Alvedi, who refused to give her consent. In a fit of desperation and heartbreak, Saamu cracked open a coconut, lit a wick in one of the halves, and placed it inside the palace. When Siri entered the palace, the flickering light of the wick dazzled her and caused an ache, and she declared that she would only enter if Saamu escorted her. It was then that Kaanebottu Ajjeru, an old man living in the palace, intervened and brought Saamu back to the Kottaradi palace. After Kodasara Alva apologized to Saamu, the first wife escorted Siri into the palace. However, the two women frequently quarrelled and displayed their magical powers, causing unrest in the palace. It was then that Kaanebottu Ajjeru, in his wisdom, brought about a truce between the two, restoring harmony to the palace.

As the seasons passed, Siri's womb grew with the promise of new life, and she was filled with an intense longing for the safety and comfort of her home. But fate had other plans, and as she made her way back from a lavish feast, Siri was struck by the sudden onset of labour pains. With no shelter in sight, she was forced to give birth right then and there, under the open sky. Yet, even in this moment of crisis, the benevolent spirit of her first-born son Kumara appeared before her in the guise of a wise brahmin. With his gentle guidance, the child was safely brought into the world. In a wondrous transformation, Kumara revealed his true form and invited Siri to join him in the realm of maya, the invisible world beyond the reach of mortal eyes. Though hesitant, Siri finally acquiesced, entrusting her newborn daughter to the care of destiny. Tenderly placing the infant on a smooth areca spathe, she watched as the little one was borne away by a sudden flood, vanishing into the ever-changing currents of life's great river.

*In certain renditions, Saamu accompanies Siri into the jungle. Kumar cautions Saamu against divulging the events that unfolded in the forest to her husband. Despite Kumar's warnings, Saamu reveals the secrets under pressure, leading to her untimely demise.

In the fullness of time, Kaanebottu Ajjeru came upon a miraculous discovery. As he strolled along the banks of a tranquil stream, he found an infant girl drifting on the gentle current. Without hesitation, he scooped her up and took her into his care. This child that he named Sonne, was welcomed into Kaanebottu Ajjeru's home, where she was raised with tenderness and love.

As fate would have it, Kaanebottu Ajjeru would soon have another child under his wing. This time, the call of destiny led him to the mouth of a dark and foreboding cave, where he heard the plaintive cries of a baby girl. With unshakeable courage, he ventured into the shadows and found the abandoned child, Gindye. He brought her to his home and raised her alongside Sonne.

In due course, Ajjeru arranged marriages for the two young women. Sonne was married to the noble Gurumarla of Urukitottu palace. However, Gindye was the first to undergo the sacred bayake ritual upon attaining puberty. Although Sonne was keen to attend the event, her husband initially forbade it. But her familial bond was too strong to be denied.

'She is my sister, and I will attend at any cost,' Sonne insisted.

'Fine,' her husband relented, 'but do not come back if you are insulted.'

Despite her husband's warning, Sonne journeyed to the ceremony, hoping to honour Gindye. Alas, the gathering took a cruel turn, as the assembled women taunted Sonne for her perceived failure at attaining puberty. She was ridiculed and mocked, and her spirit was broken. As the ceremony drew to a close, Sonne invoked her magical power and made Gindye vanish into the realm of maya, where she would be reunited with Kumara and other spirits.

As Sonne returned to her husband Gurumarla after the bayake ceremony, he could sense the humiliation she had undergone. The couple, heartbroken and filled with remorse, turned to the divine powers for guidance. They offered their prayers and made a vow to Bermer*, promising a golden offering at Nandalike if they were blessed with offspring. The divine blessings came to fruition as Sonne attained puberty and gave birth to two beautiful twin girls, Abbaga and Daaraga.

In another version, a brahmin appears in Sonne's dream and forecasts the birth of twins if she offered a gold coin.

Chapter 4 — Abbaga and Daaraga

However, as they were caught up in the joys of family life, Sonne and Gurumarla neglected their promise to Bermer. They failed to keep their word to the divine powers, much to their detriment. Bermer, appearing before them disguised as a fortune teller, cautioned them of the dire consequences that awaited them if they ignored their vow. Everything that they had been blessed with would be taken back, he warned. This occurrence was akin to the early days of our tale, when Bermer Ajjeru failed to restore the sacred shrines and thus was consumed by sorrow and desolation. Like a cycle of fate, the past repeated itself as Sonne and Gurumarla neglected their promise to Bermer after being bestowed with the gifts of twin daughters. Gurumarla, consumed by anger, rebuffed the fortune teller and commanded him to leave.

As time passed, the twins, Abbaga and Daraga, blossomed into young women, well-educated and proficient in their favourite board game of Cenne. The game board, a work of art crafted from exquisite rosewood or ebony, was adorned with small cowrie shells, an object of great fascination to the sisters. Their passion for the game grew as they did, and they often engaged in lively battles of strategy and skill.

It was during this period that the twin sisters caught the attention of Rama and Lakkanna, the twins of Boliyasandra of Kaderi Kaarla, who sought their hands in marriage. However, Gurumaarla hesitated to give his consent as their family's vow to Bermer remained unfulfilled. Though Sonne pressed him, Gurumaarla was reluctant to agree as he felt his daughters were too young for marriage. Yet, with the permission of Gurumaarla's elder brother, he eventually accepted the proposal.

Thus, Sonne and Gurumaarla set out to invite Kaanebottu Ajjeru for the twins' marriage, but the couple was not present at the palace. It was then that Bermer, taking on the guise of a poor brahmin, appeared before the sisters and lured them into playing a game of Cenne. Gurumaarla had locked the game board away due to his daughters' quarrels, but the disguised brahmin was able to access it. The game quickly turned violent, and the sisters began fighting until Abbaga, in a fit of rage, lifted the wooden board and struck Daaraga on the head, killing her instantly. Overcome with guilt, Abbaga dragged her sister's lifeless body to a nearby well and tossed it in. She then jumped into the abyss of the well herself. As soon as they went in the water, their bodies transformed into a bunch of areca flowers or pingaara. They floated on the surface, as their parents arrived, unable to find their beloved daughters.

The girls, in spirit form, then arrived at Bermer's abode, where they expressed their desire to be married. Bermer granted them three days of life in the physical world, and they returned as spirits to Urkitottu, where they encountered their parents who were still searching for them. Initially, the parents were blaming Bermer for their disappearance, but the girls reminded their parents that it was their unfulfilled vow that had led to their tragic fate.

Moving on from Urkitottu, in the scorching heat of the mid-noon, the girls assumed human form under a banyan tree in Abbanadka. They proceeded to the weddings of Rama and Lakkanna, causing the potter, the barber, the washerman, the fire worker and the drummer to vanish. When they asked a brahmin lady for water, she refused, consumed with her household chores. In response, the girls cursed that the brahmin woman would forever remain busy with chores and never find spare time. However, when a Christian woman brought flowers to the wedding, they graciously accepted and blessed her with a bountiful harvest, ensuring that her crops would always flower regardless of drought or flood.

At the wedding venue, the hum of whispers rumbled through the twin grooms like a gust of wind through leaves. The guests became aware of the absence of the washerman, the potter and the barber. Their customary services had been omitted, leaving a glaring gap in the ceremonial rituals. The guests, who had come to revel in the auspicious occasion, now found themselves troubled and disoriented. One could almost hear their mournful lament, as they mourned what could have been. They spoke in hushed tones, and pondered how Abbaga and Daaraga, if they had not succumbed to an untimely death, would have been the radiant brides, and how different the celebration would have been with them at the centre.

The sisters, Abbaga and Daaraga, arrived at the wedding venue in spirit form. They then took the form of the brides who had replaced them and attended the wedding, marrying Rama and Lakkanna. However, they soon left the bodies of the brides without waiting for the traditional milk drinking ceremony, returning to the sacred realm of spirits. As their parents had vowed to make gold offerings at Nandalike, the spirits of Abbaga and Daaraga made their way in that direction, guided by the spirit of Siri Kumara.

Notes

True Essence of the Siri Legend

The Siri legend stands for the emancipation of Tulu women and their non-violent struggle against male dominance and injustice. Siri, a woman of divine origin, experiences the typical struggles of a woman, grappling with male dominance and dictation in society. The mass possession rituals during the Siri jaatre are a performative presentation of the Siri story, predominantly through prayer recitation, reflecting the close interaction and interpretation of the spirit and human realms.

Siri Jaatre

The Siri jaatre, also known as Siri alade, is observed on the full moon night in six different temples across the region. The belief is that the siris possesses women for various reasons. Kumara, the male character in the story, serves as the male medium, conversing with the women in a trance, and encouraging them to identify with various female characters from the legend. These women enter a trance and sing Siri paaddanas. The therapeutic effect of possession may be that it provides catharsis for these participants, some of whom may be troubled domestically. Therefore, ritual is believed to offer them a safe space to temporarily cast aside their individual identities and step beyond their real-life limitations, releasing their anxieties, anger, frustrations and unfulfilled desires. They can confront the trauma inflicted upon them by family members, caste prejudices, class conflicts and general dissatisfaction.

8

Jumadi

Jumadi

In the high mountains of India, there lived a queen who was impregnated by the rays of the sun. As she neared the end of her pregnancy, she cried out in pain and agony. She feared that she might not survive such a painful ordeal. She prayed for help and relief from her suffering.

'Please, someone, help me give birth to this baby,' she cried out.

The baby inside her womb was no ordinary child. It was the child of the Sun (god) and possessed incredible powers. It spoke to its mother from within the womb and said, 'O Mother! Being the miracle that I am, I shall not come out through this passage meant for ordinary human babies.'

And so, the baby broke open the mother's womb and emerged as a spirit named Jumadi. The news of the dark-skinned baby who blasted out of its mother's womb spread like wildfire through the mountains.

One day, while Jumadi was wandering around trying to quench its thirst, it met a toddy-tapper who was returning home after setting pots under palm trees.

'I am thirsty! Give me something to drink!' Jumadi said.

'Please go to the toddy shop where my mother will give you something to quench your thirst,' the toddy-tapper said.

Jumadi was angered by this response. The next morning, the toddy-tapper found his pots filled with blood. He was heartbroken as he couldn't earn his bread that day. He informed the other members of the village council, and together they visited a sorcerer to find a solution to the problem of the new spirit.

The sorcerer offered a solution that required many sacrifices and rituals. In the end, they were able to control the spirit of Jumadi and confine it inside a bell-bronze box, which they deposited in a pond.

'This is where Jumadi will remain, confined forever,' the astrologer declared.

But fate had other plans for Jumadi. A group of soldiers arrived at the pond. They noticed a big fish and decided to catch it. One of the soldiers exclaimed, 'Hey, let's throw the net into the pond and catch this fish!'

As they threw the net, they accidentally caught the bell-bronze box containing Jumadi's spirit along with the fish. While lifting the net out of the water, the box fell on the shore, and the soldiers were intrigued by it. One of them said, 'What could be inside this box?'

'I think it is a treasure,' another one said.

'Maybe glittering gems and priceless pearls!'

'Let's carry it to the top of the hill and see what treasure it contains.'

'Whatever it is, we will share it equally,' they said in chorus.

At the top of the hill, as they opened the box, a golden bee floated out of it. The soldiers looked at each other in surprise. There was nothing else inside the box. Their hopes of finding a treasure were shattered.

The golden bee flew up until it arrived in Vaikuntha. Lord Narayana observed the shadow cast on his western side by the spirit and turned around, but he saw the bee instead.

Narayana asked the bee, 'O spirit, who are you?'

The spirit replied, 'I am Jumadi.'

Narayana asked, 'Why have you come here?'

Jumadi replied, 'I am thirsty and hungry. I want something to drink. Will you fulfill my desire?'

Narayana remarked, 'I would gladly fulfill your desire if you promise to get me my belt and japamaala from Brahma.'

Immediately, the spirit left for Brahmaloka, where it appeared in the form of a brahmin boy. Using its intelligence, Jumadi obtained the items that belonged to Narayana and came back to Vaikuntha. Impressed with the spirit, Narayana said, 'O Spirit, you can drink as much as you want from the ponds in my abode.'

Jumadi extended its tongue and it rolled out like a carpet and dipped inside the pond. It drank all the waters, but that did not quench its thirst.

'I want more,' it said.

Narayana offered elephants, but that did not quench the spirit's hunger.

'I want more,' it said.

Narayana chopped his little finger and offered it to the spirit. Jumadi transformed into a bird and sucked the blood out of it, making Narayana faint. When Narayana got up, he saw the spirit was still unsatisfied.

'More,' it said.

Finally, Narayana said, 'You are no ordinary spirit, so your thirst cannot be so ordinarily quenched. You must go down to earth and seek offerings from devotees to quench your thirst and hunger.'

Thus, Jumadi made its way to earth, arriving at the hills of Bolluru. It entered a fort where another spirit was present.

Koteda Babbu, the spirit of the fort, asked Jumadi, 'Who are you?'

Jumadi replied, 'I am Jumadi. I am thirsty. Please give me something to drink.'

Babbu brought a tender coconut, pinned a hole on it, and gave it to Jumadi. The water quenched Jumadi's thirst, and he went on to travel across Tulu Nadu, establishing itself as a powerful spirit.

Notes

The spirit of Jumadi takes many forms, including Sarala Jumadi, Marlu Jumadi, Panch Jumadi, Maley Jumadi, and others. One legend tells of a landlord named Pangalu Bannar who, beset by misfortunes, decided to he conduct a kola, or a ritualistic dance, for Jumadi. Bannar formed a committee of volunteers to collect bondas, or tender coconuts, for the kola. One villager, named Naagayya, however, refused to contribute. As per the story, this angered the spirit of Jumadi, who, in a vengeful act, caused Naagayya's niece and her newborn baby to disappear. The niece came to be known as Mayanda Mani, while the baby became a spirit called Banta. During the kola, Jumadi is always accompanied by Banta, who is believed to be a mute spirit. This evokes memories of a temple procession I attended some years ago, where performers embodying Jumadi and Banta, alongside the temple priest bearing the deity, engage in a mesmerising spectacle. It's a captivating display that immerses spectators in the essence of the annual procession.

Jumadi is said to be androgynous, being half male and half female. Some, however, claim that Jumadi may be identical to the goddess Dhumavati.

Dhumavati

Dhumavati, the seventh of the ten Mahavidya Goddesses, is believed to be an old widow associated with inauspicious and unattractive things. This goddess is known for her constant hunger and thirst, and her tendency to initiate quarrels. Dhumavati is often equated with Alakshmi and Nirritti. In her depictions, she appears as a thin, unhealthy and pale widow who wears old, dirty clothes and has disheveled hair. Unlike other Mahavidyas, she is unadorned and holds a winnowing basket in one of her trembling hands while making either boon-conferring or knowledge-giving gestures with the other.

According to legend, Parvati once felt extremely hungry while Shiva meditated in Kailasa. Despite asking him for food, he did not respond as he was engrossed in his meditation. Parvati tried to satiate her hunger, but nothing seemed to work. Out of anger, she ate Shiva, and smoke started emanating from within her body, leading to the naming of the deity as Dhumavati, which means 'the smoky one.'

Another variation of the story tells of Shiva getting stuck in Parvati's throat when she swallows him. It is said that at that moment, the couple blended into one form, and Dhumavati was born. This androgynous form of Dhumavati is believed to have defeated the demon Dhumasura, who could only be killed by a person who was both a man and a woman at the same time.

Similarities in Origin Stories

Jumadi and Dhumavati may be two distinct figures with their own unique characteristics and origins, yet they share commonalities in their depiction as dark or grey coloured, hungry and thirsty figures. Dhumavati's androgynous form portrayed in the legend is synonymous with the form depicted in the story of Jumadi. Jumadi is a folk deity revered in the Tulu-speaking regions and represents the rural, agricultural way of life, while Dhumavati is one of the ten Mahavidya goddesses in Hinduism and symbolizes the darker aspects of life such as loss, sorrow and isolation. Despite their differences, both figures offer a powerful reflection of the human experience and a means to find meaning and understanding in the face of life's challenges.

By now, you must have noticed the similarities in the origin stories of daivas. Whether Jumadi is the same Dhumavati or different cannot be known. If the queen of mountains, who gave birth to Jumadi was the same as Puranic Parvati, we may never know. Interestingly, there is another fierce spirit deity known as Guliga who shares a similar origin story as Jumadi. This can once again be attributed to variations in oral tradition. These can cause similarities in origin stories of these primordial deities due to the transmission of stories over time, adaptation by different storytellers and regions, and the use of archetypes and motifs that are common across cultures. Many of the primitive deities in India have been assimilated into the Hindu pantheon over the centuries, resulting in their stories becoming intertwined with Hindu mythology.

9

The Fearsome Spirits

WHILST RESIDING IN KARKALA, I FOUND MYSELF to be a frequent visitor to the local kolas. One night, I was speaking to one of the organizers at a kola performance when out of the blue, a kola dancer popped up and ran all around like wind in a storm. With the sudden appearance of this performer, the atmosphere was charged with electricity, as if a gust of wind had descended upon us. His visage was darkened with a coat of inky black pigment, while his wrists were encircled by bracelets and armlets woven from supple palm fronds. I decided to quietly observe the scene unfolding before me, stowing my camera away in my bag, as one of the most formidable spirits of Tulu Nadu, known as Guliga, revealed itself in all its raw intensity.

The legends tell of two sisters who sought the blessings of Lord Narayana to bear children, and Narayana promised to grant their wish the following day. However, the younger sister, fuelled by greed and envy, sneaked away to receive the boon alone, leaving behind her slumbering elder sister. Narayana, true to his word, bestowed upon her the gift of twenty-four children, but the elder sister, upon awakening and discovering her sibling's treachery, cursed her children. All but four perished in the curse, and from these survivors emerged Guliga, Jattiga, Chaundi and Rahu Guliga, terrifying spirits with a boundless thirst for destruction.

In another version of the tale, Parvati, the wife of Lord Shiva, finds a stone amid a heap of ash, and when Lord Shiva hurls it into the water, it gives rise to Guliga or Gulikan. The fierce deity is believed to be a fearsome incarnation of Lord Shiva, with a thirst for destruction so insatiable that it drains the seas and devours all the fish. Not even the blood of elephants and horses can quench its hunger. It was only when Lord Narayana offered him his little finger that Guliga's hunger subsided and his belly was full. Narayana then sent him to earth to accept offerings from the people and to keep a check on sinners. There is a version which says that Guliga was born to Vaayu and Bhadrakaali. At the time of taking birth, it rejected the traditional passage, and came out of its mother's breast.

If one travels further south to Kerala, Guliga transforms into Gulikan, a renowned deity who is prominently featured in Theyyams. Interestingly, the word 'gulika' in Malayalam literally means a tablet which might be a reference to the earliest form of idols used for the deity. One legend is associated with the sage Markandeya. When Markandeya was born, he was gifted high intellect but he would only live till the age of sixteen. In the crucible of these fleeting years, Markandeya blossomed into an unwavering devotee of Lord Shiva. As the sands of time converged upon the destined moment of his death, the yamadoothas, or grim reapers from Yamaloka, arrived to claim his soul. Yet, defying the inevitable, Markandeya clung tenaciously to the sacred Shivalinga that he had been worshipping for sixteen years. Foiled in their attempt to uproot his soul, the yamadoothas retreated to

Yamaloka. The god of death, Yama, took matters into his own hands, wielding his formidable weapon—the rope of death. The sage, resolute in his devotion, didn't let go off the Shivalinga and kept praying. Yama, undeterred, cast his deathly noose upon the young sage, only to find it ensnared around the Shivalinga. The Shivalinga transformed into ether, and from inside, Lord Shiva appeared. Consumed by wrath, Shiva opened his third eye, a fiery aperture that incinerated Yama to ashes. Thereafter, there was no death on earth, which created an imbalance, and at the request of the sages, Shiva pressed his left thumb on the ground, and from it emerged a formidable, grim reaper called Gulikan, who is then tasked with overseeing death and punishment.

Gulikan is venerated as a tutelary deity in North Kerala, particularly in the border regions of Karnataka and Kerala, where dedicated groves to Guliga are situated. These sacred locations are termed 'mundya' in Kerala. During kola rituals, members of the Koppaala community take on the persona of Guliga, symbolizing the essence and importance of this deity (Unnikrishnan, 2023, pg. no. 117).

In certain belief systems, Gulika is regarded as one of the eight principal Naagas, alongside Ananta, Vasuki, Shankhapaalaka, Takshaka, Mahaapadma, Padma, and Karkotaka. It is believed that all other serpents originated from these primary Naagas. In Vedic Astrology, Gulika or Gulikan holds a significant position. Gulikakaalam is known as an inauspicious or unfavorable time of day. Gulika is the progeny of the mighty Shanidev, representing Saturn. According to ancient lore, Gulikan's birth was accompanied by ominous events that foreshadowed the arrival of a formidable entity.

It is said that once Shani had a quarrel with Guru Brihaspati, the planetary embodiment of Jupiter. In a fit of rage, Brihaspati shot an arrow that struck Shani on the forehead. As the arrow was removed, a dark blue viscous object trickled down from the wound, and dropped on the earth. A serpent-like being appeared from the object. As soon as that happened, dark clouds filled the skies, and natural disasters began to unfold, portending the malevolent nature of the newly created entity. Vishnu, the preserver and protector of the universe, intervened and named the creation 'Gulikan'. As Shanidev was called Mandhan, his son, Gulikan came to be known as Mandhi. It is believed that Gulikan's other name, Mrityu, refers to his role in causing death and destruction.

Although the origins of Guliga are steeped in myth and legend, the similarities in his character traits and those of other fearsome spirits like Gulikan (Theyyam), Guliga and Rahu Guliga (Kola) are striking. Despite the lack of a direct link between these entities, there is no denying the clear parallelism that exists across various tales and myths from different regions.

In spirit worship of Tulu Nadu, it is not just Guliga who is considered fierce, and whose origin story is now lost. There is the vigorous Chaundi, who is feared and revered by all. In the local lore of the region, Chaundi is believed to have originated from the Ghats. During the Chaundi kola ritual, a rooster was typically offered to appease this deity in the olden times. Once the offering was made, Chaundi was said to play with the rooster like a cat playing with a mouse, before ultimately sinking its teeth into it. Interestingly, Guliga also accepts such offerings.

Alongside Guliga, other deities commonly worshipped outside homes include Rahu, Jattiga, Kshetrapala, Rakteshwari, and Chaundi, reflecting the diverse range of beliefs and practices in the area. In certain folk narratives, Kshetrapala is portrayed as the offspring of Shiva and Kaalaratri. This progeny, after vanquishing an asura, acquired the name Kshetrapala. In other traditions, Kshetrapala serves as a guardian deity who wears a serpent as a sacred thread and may also protect the mother goddess(es). In the Shiva Purana, Chamundi, Bhadrakali, Bhairava, and Kshetrapala are among the formidable fierce entities who accompany Veerabhadra and Shiva's bhutaganas to Daksha's sacrifice.

So, it is believed that when those four fearsome children were born from the woman's womb, they wreaked havoc on earth. Seeking relief from their thirst, they ascended to Vaikuntha and made a demand of Lord Narayana. But Narayana had other plans as he transformed them into powerful spirits, each with a specific duty to fulfill. Chaundi was given a bell and a stick and instructed to watch over pregnant women and cows, while Guliga was given a burning torch and tasked with keeping ghostly apparitions at bay during the night. These spirits are known to be dangerous, causing harm to those who cross them. As such, those who offer oblations to these spirits must do so with great care and devotion (Upadhyaya, 2002, p. 116-117).

Meanwhile, recollecting the incident at the kola, I witnessed the kola artist possessed by Guliga in a frenzied state, his body contorting and writhing as he danced. Upon noticing individuals attempting to capture his image, he emitted a disapproving groan, prompting them to hastily stow their phones away in their pockets. Suddenly, he made a break for it, attempting to run away from the chappara. The votaries quickly sprang into action, forming a circle around him to prevent his escape. It was a chaotic and intense moment, with the wild dancer struggling against the restraining circle of devotees, their voices raised in a fevered pitch as they tried to subdue the possessed performer. I had never witnessed anything so intense before.

However, there exists another deity known as Mookambi Guliga, whose kola is even more intense. On the occasion of this kola, hundreds of logs are stacked together, and dried areca nut palms are cut down to create a heap. This heap is then ignited into flames. Amidst the fiery inferno, the kola artist, believed to be possessed by the spirit of Mookambi Guliga, enters the flames, rolling, sitting, and lying within the burning pyre. The photograph adorning the cover of this book features the kola dancer embodying Mookambi Guliga.

The legend behind the Mookambi Guliga kola starts with Guliga, who settled down at Maranakatte, where the goddess Mookambika annihilated Mookasura. With the grace of the goddess, Guliga was given the form of Brahmalingeshwara. It is said that the goddess had issued instructions to perform the puja of Guliga on the right side of Mookasura.

Once, a Tantri (Thanthri) from Kollur set out for Kerala with his wife, Mookambika, to perform a Shanti puja. Guliga daiva accompanied the Tantri to Kerala to protect him. On the way, a person tried to molest the Tantri's wife. She was so shocked by this heinous act that she ended her life by jumping into the water. In the spirit realm, her soul merged with that of Guliga daiva. Unified, the spirits, now known as Mookambi Guliga, exacted vengeance by annihilating the entire family of the perpetrator. Since that fateful day, the amalgamated spirit has been revered as Mookambi Guliga, considered one of the most potent deities.

10

Kordabbu and Thanimaaniga

Chapter 1 — Birth of Babbu

IN THE LAND OF TULU NADU, WHERE THE SUN shines bright and the winds whisper secrets, there lived a woman named Kachurmalthi. Her heart was pure and her spirit strong, but fate was not kind to her. She gave birth to a baby boy, but soon after, both she and her husband passed away, leaving the child alone in the world.

The baby's cries echoed through the village, and it reached the ears of a kind neighbour, Kodange Bannar. Moved by the child's plight, Bannar approached the baby. As he neared, a bright light flashed in front of him, and he heard the voice of the mother's spirit say to him, 'You must look after my son!'

As soon as the baby was placed in Bannar's lap, it smiled at him, as if it had found its guardian. Bannar, being a kind soul, took the baby to his sister's house, who had longed for a child of her own.

They raised the baby with immense love and care and named him Babbu. However, Babbu was not an ordinary child; he possessed the power to perform miracles.

One day, Babbu's foster mother left some grains for drying in the front yard. However, hens from their home and the neighbouring homes kept coming and stealing the grains. The foster mother, annoyed with the situation, asked Babbu to keep an eye on the hens and shoo them away. Few minutes later, a hen appeared and when Babbu saw it, he threw a stick at it and it died.

Hours later, when the foster mother returned, she was dismayed to see all the hens dead in the front yard. She was upset as they were dependent on the hens, and she had only asked Babbu to shoo them away, not to kill them. Babbu comforted her and threw another stick at the birds, and miraculously, all of them came back to life. Thus, he was bestowed with a new name, Kordabbu.

As Babbu continued to grow and develop his remarkable gifts for prophecy and divination, his name began to spread far and wide. He could tell where to dig a well to find plentiful water. However, as is often the case with those who achieve great renown, there were those who saw his rise as a threat and conspired against him. One day, they kidnapped his beloved cow and cast it into a nearby river, hoping to end Babbu's power and influence once and for all. When Babbu arrived on the scene, he was met with the grim sight of his cow being devoured by a ferocious crocodile. But rather than give up hope, Babbu used his mystical abilities to resurrect the animal, breathing new life into it and proving his power to all who witnessed the miracle. He was known as Vaidyanatha from then onwards.

But even this wondrous feat was not enough to win over all of Babbu's detractors. There was a powerful king in the nearby region of Katpaadi who viewed Babbu with great suspicion and envy. Seeking to rid himself of this upstart challenger, the king cunningly invited Babbu to his court, ostensibly to perform a feat of magic and produce water from a long-dry well. Despite his misgivings, Babbu agreed to the task, but soon found himself in a trap—the king's men had covered the well with a heavy stone slab, leaving Babbu trapped and alone at the bottom. His calls for help went unanswered, and it seemed that his enemies had finally succeeded in their plot to silence him forever.

In the verdant forest, as fate would have it, Thannimaaniga chanced upon the well, where a voice cried for help. The fair maiden peered down and saw a man trapped inside.

'Who are you?' she inquired.

'I am Babbu. The king and his men trapped me inside, please help me get out. If you are a male then I shall call you my brother, if you are a female, I shall forever call you my sister,' Babbu replied in a distressed voice.

Thannimaaniga immediately removed the slab that covered the well and searched for a rope to pull Babbu out. But none was found. She then had an idea and told Babbu, 'I will remove my saree and throw it down. You can hold it to come up. However, you must swear not to look at my bare body when you climb up.'

'I give my word, sister!'

Babbu readily agreed and soon used the saree to climb out of the well. But as he emerged from the dark abyss, his eyes inadvertently fell on Thannimaaniga's bare chest, breaking the promise he had made to her. Thannimaaniga was incensed, and Babbu was filled with deep remorse and regret.

To atone for his mistake, Babbu took a sword and struck his forehead sixteen times until it bled. He then fell at Thannimaaniga's feet, begging for her forgiveness. Moved by his sincerity, Thannimaaniga forgave and then blessed him.

Chapter 2—Daivaraja Babbu Swamy

Bobbarya was a powerful spirit of the sea who longed to be recognized and revered by the people of the land. His desire to be known was so strong that he decided to take matters into his own hands. One day, as the kingly spirits or Rajan Daivas were making their way to a river to take a dip, they encountered Bobbarya blocking their path.

The Rajan Daivas, who held themselves in high esteem, were not willing to pay heed to Bobbarya's request for recognition. Bobbarya, who grew in size, placed one foot on the ghats and the other foot on the sea. The Rajan Daivas felt insulted and told Bobbarya to move out of their way. Bobbarya, however, challenged them to move him if they could. The Rajan Daivas would be belittled if they had to pass under the groin of the giant Bobbarya.

The Rajan Daivas tried to use their powers, but it was of no use against Bobbarya's might. Frustrated, they implored a spirit named Babbu Swami to intervene and promised to elevate his status if he could move Bobbarya. Babbu Swami tried to reason with Bobbarya, but he remained obstinate.

Provoked by Bobbarya's belligerence, Babbu Swami's calm demeanour gave way to a fierce form. With one swift strike, Babbu Swami cut Bobbarya's foot, clearing the path for the Rajan Daivas to continue on their way. The Rajan Daivas were pleased with Babbu Swami's display of strength and bestowed upon him a unique position among the spirits of Tulu Nadu, that of Daivaraja.

Bobbarya, filled with remorse for his actions, pleaded for forgiveness from Babbu Swami. The blood that dripped from Bobbarya's broken leg was symbolic of his ego, which Babbu Swami forgave. Using his powers, Babbu Swami healed Bobbarya's leg, living up to the title of Vaidyanatha, the master of medicines.

Thus, Kordabbu, also known as Daivaraja Babbu Swami, became a legend in Tulu Nadu, admired and revered by all. His story was passed down from generation to generation, reminding the people of the power of forgiveness and the importance of recognizing the worth of all beings, no matter how small or insignificant they may seem. In some variations, Koraga Taniya or Pilichandi also confront Bobbarya with Babbu Swami.

Notes

I heard the story of Thannimaaniga and Kordabbu from multiple sources. Some believe that Thannimaaniga was the incarnation of the goddess Parvati herself.

On the other hand, Kordabbu's story reflects the harsh realities of social discrimination and marginalization. Kordabbu is depicted as a boy from an erstwhile lower community who met an untimely demise due to societal injustices. Despite his humble origins, Kordabbu's transformation into a spirit after death, known as Babbu Swami or Koteda Babbu, highlights his resilience and significance within the cultural narrative.

During the kola dance, one artist assumes the persona of Kordabbu, wearing male attire, while the other portrays Thannimaaniga in female attire. The artist portraying Kordabbu symbolically taps his head with a sword. Kordabbu and Thannimaaniga are revered as sibling spirits during the ceremony.

11

Bobbarya

ONCE UPON A TIME, THERE WAS A MAN NAMED Murava Byari. He lived in a village where a Jain girl was in distress because all her bridegrooms were killed by a serpent that came out of her nose at midnight. Murava Byari came to the village to offer himself as the bridegroom. He made a human replica of rice powder paste and kept it by the bride's side. At midnight, a cobra came out of the bride's nose, but Murava killed it and married her.

Murava and his wife had a son, Bappa, who went on a shipping expedition with his followers. However, the ship was wrecked in a cyclone or while engaged in a maritime battle. Bappa was the only survivor, but he was transformed into a spirit, known as Bobbarya, the guardian of the seas.

The spirit of Bobbarya took rest at Mulur, near Kaup. One day, a toddy-tapper came that way and was blessed by the spirit, but he was not supposed to disclose the secret to anyone. He got extraordinary yield that day. Unable to control his urge to spill the secret, the toddy-tapper shared it with his wife. This angered the spirit. As a result, the toddy-tapper got only blood in his toddy pot the next day, and when he went to clean his knife near the lotus pond, he was immersed in the water.

The rumour of the new spirit spread like wildfire. In order to pacify the spirit, the people constructed a shrine and arranged periodical festivals. Bobbarya was worshipped in a pillar-like structure with a platform of stone serving as the altar. A pyramid-shaped stone, called daanya, was kept as its weapon. The fishermen community celebrated Bobbarya with a wooden mace in different parts of the coastal region.

Origins & Controversy

The above story is based on a paaddana translated by Burnell. While the genesis of most daivas is steeped in mystery, the origin of Bobbarya is shrouded in controversy. Given the lack of conclusive evidence, some have dismissed the commonly floated origin story of Bobbarya being born to a Muslim man and Jain woman as unsubstantiated hearsay.

Bobbarya is revered as the guardian deity of the Mogaveera community and the chief protector of their fishing expeditions. According to this alternate origin story, he is thought to have been derived or incarnated from Babruvahana, the son of Pandava prince Arjuna and his wife, Pramila.

In the Mahabharata, Babruvahana was the son of Arjuna and Chitrangada. However, in Jaimini's version, there is a mention of Pramila, the princess from Naripura, who captures the sacrificial horse that Arjuna was chasing. He marries her and continues to pursue the horse. Then, the sacrificial horse enters Manipura, where the grown-up Babruvahana captures the horse, before entering a battle with his father.

It is difficult to say which one is the correct one, nevertheless, Bobbarya remains a powerful and popular deity who guards those in the sea.

Before going on a fishing expedition or taking to the sea, the people pray to Bobbarya for protection and a safe return to the shore. In 2019, when seven fishermen went missing in Malpe, the community turned to Bobbarya daiva, their revered deity, for help. At a gathering, the daiva entered the body of the Patri (impersonator medium) and conveyed a message to the fishermen's families. The daiva assured them that the missing fishermen were safe but had been captured by people outside the state.

12

The Royal Deities

Kodamanithaya

IN DAYS OF YORE, THERE DWELT A MAN WHO, UPON returning from his ablutions in the river, chanced upon the voice of a spirit. 'I would like to accompany you,' spoke the spirit. The man, magnanimous in spirit, replied, 'I have no authority to impede your passage. If it be your wish, you may follow in my wake.' Thus, the spirit trailed the man back to his village.

In this bucolic village, agriculture was the mainstay. A young cowherd boy was entrusted with the arduous task of tending the cattle. Every night, the crops would be laid waste by a marauding buffalo. The landowner chided the boy for his failure to discharge his duty, and according to some accounts, he was severely punished. Determined to catch the miscreant, the boy laid in wait. When he finally espied the buffalo, he gave chase, brandishing a stick. The buffalo, sprinting towards a pond, leapt into its depths, with the boy in hot pursuit.

Lo and behold, the boy had unwittingly crossed the threshold into the netherworld, where he bore witness to a breathtaking golden edifice, belonging to a divine being. The deity conferred upon the boy a bronze bell and other objects, declaring that if he kept them close, he would beget great prosperity. However, there was one condition—he must not disclose the secret behind his success. The boy vowed to keep the covenant, and returned to his village with the bell, his fortune suddenly changing for the better.

As word of his newfound wealth spread, the villagers were agog with curiosity, but their attitudes towards him also changed. One day, his wife begged him to reveal the source of their sudden affluence. Believing that his wife was to be trusted, he divulged the secret. Alas, the boy had broken his vow, and the deity, angered by his transgression, banished him to the realm of maya. Not long after, his wife also departed from their home.

Strange and wondrous events soon began to transpire in the vicinity. Villagers reported hearing the mellifluous jingle of a 'gaggara' at night, serpents and mongooses playing together, and a leopard and cow coexisting harmoniously in a field. All were convinced that a divine spirit had descended upon their land. Two asranars (priests) were summoned to decipher these portents, and through their astrological knowledge, they determined that a sacred deity had come to reside in their village. However, they must construct a sthaana to placate the deity's ire. And so, they welcomed Rajan Daiva Kodamanithaya into the pantheon of Tulu Nadu's venerated spirits.

Dugganna of Ekkar and Timmantikari of Tibar were synonymous with two things—expertise in cock-fighting and knowledge of bullocks. Once, they visited the Durga Parameshwari temple in Iruvail, and made some offerings to the revered goddess. The next day, they ascended the ghats and procured a fine cock and a bullock that caught their fancy. Subsequently, they tied both animals to a post that they had erected under a peepal tree.

As they were walking away, they suddenly heard cries and groans emanating from the direction of the post. Alarmed, they immediately turned back to investigate and were left awestruck. The bullock was possessed by Kodamanithaya, and the cock by the spirit of Perinja. Sensing that powerful spirits had made their presence felt, the duo made haste and travelled to the village of Berke in Tangadi, carrying the bullock and the cock with them.

After arriving at Berke, Dugganna and Timmantikari constructed two gudis, one each for the spirits of Kodamanataya and Perinja. Kodamanataya demanded that not just a gudi but a palace should be erected for him, which proved to be a Herculean task, as a pillar worked on by three hundred men shattered into pieces. In a strange twist of fate, the trees between the villages of Perinja in the east and Derinja hill in the west started shedding their fruit, a sign that Kodamanataya's wishes must be granted. Eventually, both a gudi and a palace were built, and the spirit of Perinja demanded that a flag-raising ceremony in honour of Narayana should be performed, which made him known as a daiva in the village, firmly establishing his presence there.

Notes

Verily, Kodamanithaya, one of the Rajan Daivas of Tulu Nadu, is a revered spirit with a widespread following. His shrines in Yekkar, Shivarur, Uppinangadi and Perinje are known far and wide. Adorned in ornate ani and jewellry, Kodamanithaya's royal background is apparent. It is believed that the origin of this Rajan Daiva is from

Belthangadi, but as time passed, his glory spread across the district, marking his presence everywhere. Kodamanithaya is addressed by several names such as Kodamandaya, Kodamantaya, Kudamantaya, Kodamantaya and Kumbha Kanthini. As an offering, he is served vegetarian food, and his cart or bandi is symbolized by a tiger.

The Rajan Daivas are revered spirits often linked with royal or noble lineage, historically favoured by the ruling class. Kodamanitaaya, Jaarandaaya, Todakukkinaar, Jumadi, Ullaaya, and others are believed to resonate within this esteemed category.

Jaarandaaya

Another revered royal deity is Jaarandaaya. The popular belief is that this deity originated from Shiva. The story goes like this—

In the mists of time, when Lord Shiva was in deep meditation atop the majestic peak of Kailasa, there came a horde of wicked beings who sought to disturb his tranquil state. The disturbance provoked the lord of destruction to take action, and in his fury, he thrashed his unbound, twisted locks on the ground. From that tumultuous impact emerged a fearsome apparition, the warrior Veerabhadra. His visage was so terrifying that the wicked beings scampered away in fright, leaving the tranquil peak in peace once more. Veerabhadra, having fulfilled his duty, approached Lord Shiva and asked for further instruction.

'My dear Veerabhadra,' Shiva replied, 'I command you to relinquish your fearsome form and adopt a calm one. Descend from Kailasa and take up residence on Earth, where you shall protect my devotees and uphold the tenets of truth and righteousness. Take on the form of Jaarandaaya and perform your miraculous deeds there.'

And so it was that Veerabhadra assumed the form of Jaarandaaya and set out for Earth.

Jaarandaaya Arrives on Earth

The spirit of Jaarandaaya finds his vessel in a humble rock, caught in the unyielding grasp of earthly terrain of Tulu Nadu. Cast aside by one person, it finds refuge in the hands of another—an unwitting woman drawn to its curious allure. She decides to gift it to her brother who could use the rock to grind areca nuts.

Thus, the stone takes up residence in his abode, its true nature lying dormant until stirred by the dreams of the slumbering man. In the realm of Swapna or dreams, Jaarandaaya reveals himself as Veerabhadra, the deity descended to Earth, seeking shelter within the stone now nestled in the man's home. With promises of boundless fortune and favour, the divine pact between mortal and spirit is forged, marking the genesis of Jaarandaaya's veneration.

Jaarandaaya from Burnell's MS

Jaarandaaya arrived at the Atrel ferry, astride a white steed and holding a white umbrella, and requested the ferryman Kanya to bring the boat forth.

But Kanya demurred. 'I am not the owner of the boat, and I am not due any fare. The boat belongs to Koje Bale, who uses it for crossings on Tuesdays and Sundays.'

Jaarandaaya paid no heed. 'It matters not who owns the boat or for what purpose. I shall pay you the fare. Bring the boat to this side.'

At once, Kanya brought the boat over, and Jaarandaaya stepped aboard. 'I am headed to a village where tender coconuts and milk are in abundance,' he informed Kanya.

As the boat crossed the river, it began to spin uncontrollably. Jaarandaaya seized the opportunity to slay Kanya and then proceeded to take possession of the bodies of Koje Bale, a weeping child, and a lowing calf.

Baffled by the strange turn of events, Koje Bale summoned an astrologer, who consulted his prasna-book and discovered that a spirit named Jaarandaaya had arrived from the south.

A buffalo and its calf were offered to Jaarandaaya. A flag in honour of Vishnu, with the figure of Garuda on it, was raised and a grand feast was held. The gudi overflowed with lamps, and the courtyard was filled with people. And thus, the Daiva Jaarandaaya became firmly established in that place.

Notes

Notably, Jaarandaaya is a saatvik spirit revered as a Rajan Daiva by the feudatory chiefs and worshiped. As per some folk beliefs, he is the calm form of Veerabhadra. However, the veneration of Veerabhadra, the fierce and wrathful attendant of Lord Shiva, extends beyond his well-established presence in the Hindu pantheon. Intriguingly, his worship flourishes in the coastal Karnataka and Kerala, where he occupies a unique position within the local religious landscape.

Veerabhadra in Purana

In ancient India, there was a time when the world was ruled by kings, and gods walked amongst the mortals. Amongst them was a king named Daksha, a son of the creator god Brahma, and leader of all men. He was a powerful king, with armies of warriors at his command and a vast kingdom under his rule. But, he had a problem. His daughter, Sati, was in love with the god Shiva, who lived a simple life atop the holy Mount Kailasa.

Daksha was not happy with this match and wanted to marry Sati off to a wealthy and noble prince who could bring him more power and wealth. However, Sati was determined to marry Shiva. She was deeply devoted to him and knew that he was her true love. But her father was not going to make it easy for her.

One day, Daksha announced a grand ceremony called a swayamvara, where many suitors would compete for Sati's hand in marriage. Daksha invited all the gods except Shiva, hoping to push his daughter towards a more suitable husband. Sati was heartbroken when she learned that Shiva was not invited. She knew that he was her true love and that no one else could compare to him.

During the ceremony, Sati held a garland for her chosen husband and threw it into the air, calling upon Shiva to receive it, even though he wasn't present. To everyone's surprise, Shiva appeared and claimed the garland, angering Daksha but forcing him to accept the marriage.

Once, Daksha held a yagna, a sacred fire ceremony, and once again did not invite Shiva or Sati. Sati felt insulted and insisted on attending. Shiva believed that she should not attend a yajna where she was not invited. However, Sati believed that as Daksha's favourite daughter, she did not need an invitation. Shiva tried to persuade her not to go, but Sati was determined. She convinced Shiva to allow her to attend with his mount, Nandi.

As they approached the yagna, the atmosphere changed. The air was thick with smoke from the sacred fire, and the scent of burning wood and ghee filled their nostrils. The sound of chanting priests and the clanging of bells echoed through the air that was filled with the fragrant scent of the flowers and incense sticks.

Soft whispers and the rustle of silk filled the atmosphere. The music of the veena and the sound of the bells created a melodious background for the event. The golden hue of the fire, blazing in the centre of the gathering, illuminated the faces of the distinguished guests and dignitaries from all over the world.

But amidst all this grandeur and festivity, a storm was brewing. When Sati and Nandi entered the yagna, all eyes were on them. King Daksha, the host of the yajna, was fuming with rage. His beautiful daughter, Sati, had defied him yet again by marrying the man of her choice, the reclusive Shiva. Daksha had not invited Shiva to the yajna, hoping to insult him and his way of life.

'Why wasn't my husband and I invited to the yajna?' Sati asked.

Daksha reacted furiously and insulted her husband's way of living in front of all the guests and dignitaries. 'Of all these noble gods and kings present here, you chose to marry a man who holds a pot of skull, smears his body with ashes, wears an animal's skin, has a garland of heads on his neck, always stays in the smashaans. What kind of a man is he?' Daksha sneered. 'I can't invite such a man to my yajna.'

Sati's eyes flashed with anger and hurt at her father's words. 'You mock Shiva and his ways. Shiva is the Lord of all creation, including these gods and sages whom you have invited here. They wouldn't be what they are if it hadn't been for Shiva,' she retorted. 'By my curse, your yajna will not bear fruit as it will be destroyed by Shiva!'

The guests and dignitaries looked on in shock and horror as Sati, unable to bear the humiliation any longer, threw herself into the sacrificial fire. They tried to save her, but it was too late. Her body was consumed by the flames.

The silence that followed was suffocating. The only sound that could be heard was the crackling of the flames. Daksha's face was ashen with terror, but a horror of gigantic proportions was yet to arrive. The gods and sages present at the yajna were aghast at the turn of events. They knew that Sati's curse would come to pass, and that Shiva would wreak havoc on the world.

When Shiva came to know about this, he was enraged. In his rage, Lord Shiva created a fierce deity named Veerabhadra from the tip of his 'jata'. Bhadrakali was also created in the process as the fierce female power. Veerabhadra had a thousand heads, a thousand arms and a thousand feet, and he carried numerous weapons in his hands. His fiery visage blazed like the sun itself, and his form rose way up into the sky.

Veerabhadra bowed before Lord Shiva and asked, 'What are my orders?'

'Go and destroy Daksha's yajna,' was the reply.

Veerabhadra left for the sacrifice, creating several other demons to aid him in the task of destruction. This fierce army trooped to Daksha's house and proceeded to destroy everything there. The skies turned black, storms raged all around, rivers flooded and the mountains shook and trembled with their roars.

The devas and the sages who had come to attend the yajna did not know what to do. They merely stood there and saw everything was thrashed. The offerings that had been piled up for the yajna were scattered here and there by Veerabhadra and his army. Daksha tried to run away, but Veerabhadra grabbed him and beheaded him with a slice of his sword.

Brahma and the other gods started to pray to Veerabhadra and his companions. 'Who are you?' they asked. 'Whoever you are, please be pacified. Please listen to our prayers and spare us.'

'Don't pray to me,' replied Veerabhadra. 'I am merely an instrument of the great Shiva. If you must pray, pray to Shiva himself.'

The gods and the sages started to pray to Lord Shiva, and he appeared to set things right. He restored the surroundings to what they used to be before Veerabhadra's destruction began. Lord Shiva also revived Daksha by mounting the head of a goat on the dead king's body. Daksha too started to pray to him and Lord Shiva obtained his due respect. However, he had to return to Kailasa with the flaming body of Sati. It is believed that parts of her body fell where Shiva was wandering, and the spots where they fell are now the 51 Shakti Peethas.

Notes

In various accounts, the genesis of the formidable deity Veerabhadra is depicted in different ways. One narrative speaks of his origin during a later era when Shiva was married to Parvati and Daksha was reborn as the son of Prachetas (Varuna) and Marisha. However, tales of his fierce birth from Shiva's jata, or matted hair, and destruction of the yajna of Daksha, coexist.

Another belief states that Veerabhadra was born from the sweat of Shiva, who was grieving over the death of his consort Sati. This perspiration fell upon the earth and gave rise to the fearsome deity, who proceeded to destroy the sacrifice. Eventually, Shiva intervened and pacified Veerabhadra, who was then appointed as the planet Mars, known as Angaraka in Hindu astrology.

If you go further south, in the state of Kerala, Veerabhadra is revered as a potent deity with temples dedicated to his worship. The theyyam ritual dance form associated with Veerabhadra is known for its awe-inspiring and fierce portrayal of the deity.

13

Mother Goddess

IN SHAKTISM, SHE IS REVERED AS THE PARA-BRAHMAN, the Supreme being. The Devi Bhagavata Purana describes her as the singular cause of the entire universe, encompassing all that is seen and unseen. She is the embodiment of Maya, assuming myriad forms, and is the ultimate source of all creation. Even the most revered gods pale in comparison to one-hundred thousandth of her divine magnitude. Many feminine spirit deities are believed to have sprung forth from Shakti, the primal Mother Goddess.

In the regional folklore of Tulu Nadu, the mother goddess holds significant importance. Indeed, as we journey towards Northern Kerala, a kinship emerges between Malabari folklore and the legends of Tulu Nadu. Here, the mother goddess, Bhagavathi, assumes various forms such as Chamundi, Raktachamundi, Rakteshwari, and Achchi, each fierce and powerful, engaged in battles against evil entities like Darika. These formidable deities hold a parallel significance in Theyyam rituals, where performers don intricate costumes akin to Kola, transforming themselves into representations of the mother goddesses. The rhythmic cadence of chenda drums and the resplendent red and orange hues of the costumes imbue these ceremonies with an entrancing aura, purportedly serving to appease the goddesses and ward off malevolent influences. They offer a profound window into the enduring faith and rich cultural heritage of the region, highlighting the deep connection between Tulu and Malayalee folk beliefs. Some of the venerated mother goddesses in the region are Ullalthi, Rakteshwari (Lakkessiri), Mariyamma, Mayindal, Sathyadevathe, etc.

Rakteshwari

Rakteshwari, a revered deity of Tulu Nadu, is believed to be synonymous with Lakkesiri, according to local lore. One version of the story suggests that a man called Balusenava found a lemon floating in the sea while dispersing his parents' bones, and on his journey back home, he visited many a temple at Udupi and Padbidri. After crossing Mangalore, he entered Kerala, where he took a nap. During the sleep, the spirit of Rakteshwari visited him in a dream, urging him to build a place of worship. The deity demanded a special tall ani and vegetarian offerings instead of blood-stained ones. In another version, Balusenava, on his way back home, stopped at Koteswara temple where the annual festivities were taking place. As he received the prasaada, he heard the voice of Rakteswari which instructed him to construct a dwelling for the spirit to reside.

In Shaktism, Rakteshwari is revered as Durga Parameshwari, an embodiment of Adi Parasakti, or the Mother Goddess. The Kateel temple in Tulu Nadu venerates Durga Parameshwari within its sanctorum, while a rock embodies Rakteshwari outside. The deity is believed to have the power to heal mental blockages, such as fear and anxiety, in devotees. I was informed that in some places, Rakteshwari is associated with cattle owners, as she is believed to safeguard newborn calves.

Sathyadevathe

Sathyadevathe, also known as Posappe, Posabhuta, or Hosabhuta, is an androgynous deity, where the prefix 'hosa' or 'posa' signifies newness. Their upper body is male, while the lower body is female. During the kola dance, the artist is bare-chested above the waist but drapes a saree below the waist to symbolize the deity. Sathyadevathe represents the all-encompassing Mother Goddess and is worshipped within the confines of the household. Her weapon is a beththa (wand), and she wears a crown resembling the radiant rays of the sun. Mallige flowers are offered to Sathyadevathe, believed to be her favourite.

While the precise origin story remains elusive, legend has it that four men embarked on a quest to build a boat. One morning, after their respective routines, they convened to deliberate on the source of wood. With each advocating for a different direction, their discussions persisted until they unanimously agreed upon a single course: southward (present day Kerala).

After consuming the previous night's rice for breakfast, they packed provisions for their journey and set off southward with their tools in tow. Upon reaching a forest abundant with trees, they discovered a magnificent specimen suitable for their boat. Its roots delved deep into the netherworld while its branches reached skyward, boasting impressive strength. However, their attempts to fell the tree were futile as their axes failed to even scratch its bark. Faced with this predicament, the men turned to prayer, making a parakke (solemn vow in English/mannat in

Hindi/nercha in Malayalam) to offer portions of the tree to sacred temples if it would fall. Miraculously, the tree toppled of its own accord. Recognizing the power of the spirit, the men invited it to accompany them home, pledging to venerate it and fashion a cot from the same wood. As it was a new unknown spirit, she was called Posabhuta. In an alternate version, the deity was already present in their home, and they beseeched her to bring down the tree. Posabhuta has been interpreted in various ways, with some viewing her as a manifestation of Bhadrakaali, while a few draw parallels with Kallurti due to similarities in the makeup worn by kola dancers. As Sathyadevathe, she is depicted as a benevolent deity in her idol form, yet transforms into a fierce figure during the kola ritual. During the performance, the dancer executes vigorous somersaults and rolls on the ground, embodying the deity's ferocity. During the kola ceremony, a tender coconut is typically selected, upon which the face of a woman is artfully drawn. This adorned coconut represents Sathyadevathe's sister and is reverentially placed in the kodiyadi, adding a symbolic dimension to the ritualistic proceedings.

Interestingly, while this aspect of daiva worship may seem distinct, the concept of 'Satyadevta' also appears in Tibetan Buddhism, where it refers to a group of guardian deities fulfilling various roles. Some like Manjusri Bodhisattva and Avalokitesvara Bodhisattva exhibit serene countenances while others, like Vajrabhairava and Haigreeva, appear fierce and formidable.

It wouldn't be an exaggeration to acknowledge the profound influence of Sathyadevathe throughout my journey. As a descendant of migrant Tuluvas, separated from our ancestral land by five generations, the worship of the daiva remained an enigma to me. However, my journey took a transformative turn upon reaching my spouse's ancestral home in Karkala. In that house, aged perhaps a century or more, a dimly lit pooja room beckoned, where the ceiling was so low that my head easily touched it. After offering my respects to the gods, I prepared to exit when I was gently instructed by the elders to pause and turn around. There, I was introduced to Varte and Sathyadevathe, revered figures enshrined on a swinging cot within their sacred chamber. It marked my initiation into the ancient customs of my forefathers—a pivotal step into a realm beyond the mundane.

Acknowledgements

IN HEARTFELT GRATITUDE, I MUST FIRST CREDIT MY mother for her unwavering dedication in speaking to me in the Tulu language, even while growing up in a distant land where no one else spoke it. Her persistent efforts throughout my childhood have afforded me the ability to speak and understand my mother tongue fluently today. Hats off to such parents who have preserved their culture through their children.

I am also indebted to my wife for introducing me to Varthe and Satyadevathe at her ancestral home in Karkala. Her steadfast faith in the 'Satyolu' has provided me with the courage to explore the world of spirit worship.

Furthermore, I must express my deep appreciation to my commissioning editor, Prerna, for understanding the concept and providing me with this divine opportunity to pen something in honour of the Daivas and folktales of Tulu Nadu.

My father, who embodies an unwavering dedication to reason and rationality, deserves a great deal of credit for shaping my worldview and providing me with the necessary tools to approach life in a practical and objective manner.

A heartfelt thank you to Shashank Nellithaya, the esteemed madhyasthar from Puttur who has officiated in thousands of kolas in two decades, who generously devoted his time to clear my doubts and happily took me to the kolas he officiated in the thenkayi region. I would also like to express my appreciation to the young prodigies, Vignesh Pejathaya and Srinivas Asranar, for graciously sharing their insights from the realm of daivas despite their busy schedules.

A special thanks to my father-in-law, whose good reputation with people helped me find the contacts needed to fuel my initial research. I offer my sincere acknowledgment here—Rahul Shastri, Vedakka, Vasanthi akka, Ganesha Moolya & family, Dhanush Gowda & family, Vikki akka, Vijeth anna, Ramanand Rao & family, Prabhakar Rao & family, and Yathi. Special thanks to Renuka Dodda and Vedu Chikappa for their warm hospitality, and to Shashi Aunty and Ammu for their invaluable assistance with Kannada translation.

Reflecting the cause and effect dynamics often depicted in the Puranas, gratitude to Ranveer Allahbadia, whose probing questions unknowingly reignited my curiosity, prompting me to embark on this journey anew. Also, to Shrutesh, Sanchit, and the entire team behind the podcast.

Thanks to the efforts of all writers and scholars who have contributed to research in this field. The likes of Burnell, Manner, Sturrock, Thurston, Susheela and UP Upadhyaya, Gururaj Bhat, Chinappa Gowda, Peter Claus, Viveka Rai, Amrita Someshwar, Babu Amin, P. Padmanabha, etc. whose works I have referred during my research.

Acknowledgements

The writer's journey, like life itself, is a winding path filled with unexpected turns. We traverse stretches of self-doubt, yearning for a helping hand that sometimes doesn't materialize, even from those we hold close. It is no different when I am writing a book of such magnitude. Yet, through it all, there is a sacred force that refuses to let me surrender, and eventually, someone appears and provides that gentle nudge in the right direction. My deepest gratitude goes out to these unexpected helpers, both seen and unseen.

My gratitude to my publisher, Udayan Mitra, and everyone at HarperCollins for their continued belief in my humble attempts at discovering the supernatural and the extraordinary.

A heartfelt thank you to bestselling author Amish Tripathi for taking the time to read this book and for sharing such encouraging words about it.

I reserve my final expression of gratitude for the Daivas and Naagas of Tulu Nadu, who, I believe, watch over me from the sacred realm of the spirits.

Bibliography

Bhat, G. P. (1975). Studies in Tuluva History & Culture. Mangalore.

Ciccarelli, S.K., Misra, G., White, N.J. (2018). Psychology, Pearson Education

P. S. Subrahmanya Sastri, M. B. (1946). Brhat Samhita of Varahamihira - Vol. 1: With English Translation, Exhaustive Notes and Literary Comments. Bengaluru: V.B Soobbiah and sons.

Iyer, N. C. (1884). The Brihat Samhita of Varaha Mihira. Madurai: South Indian Press.

Thurston, E. (1909). Castes and Tribes of Southern India. Government Press, Madras.

Burnell, A.C. (1894, 1879). The Devil Worship of the Tuluvas, Indian Antiquary

The forty-sixth report of the Basel German Evangelical missionary society in South-Western India for 1885. (1886) (p. 16). Mangalore: Basil Mission Press.

BIBLIOGRAPHY

Dr. U.P. Upadhyaya, Dr. (Smt). Upadhyaya S.P. (2002). Folk Rituals. Udupi: Regional Resources Centre for Folk Performing Arts.

Ishii, M. (2020). Modernity and Spirit Worship in India

Carrin, M. (2018). When Fearful Ghosts are Married in Tulunadu

Dhabolkar, N. (2018). The Case for Reason, Westland

Nandavara, Dr. V. (2015). Koti Chennaya - A Folkloristic Study, Karnataka Tulu Sahitya Academy

Gowda, C. (2005). The Mask and the Message, Madipu Prakashana

Rai, V. (1996). Epics in the Oral Genre System of Tulunaadu

Poojary, O.S.D. (2016). Spirit Possession and Other Stories, Karnataka Tulu Sahitya Academy

Padmanabha, P. (1975). Census of India - 1971 (Special Study Report on Bhuta Cult in South Kanara District)

Claus, P.J. (1979). Myth and Possession Cult of Tulu Naad, Asian Folklore Studies

Lauri, H. (1998). Textualising the Siri Epic, Finnish Academy of Science and Letters

Amin, B.B. (2016). Daiva Nele, Kemmalaje Janapada Prakashana (Kannada)

Amin, B.B. (2016). Daivagalamadilalli - Folklore Collection, Kemmalaje Janapada Prakashana (Kannada)

Padre, N.S. (2022). Kaaranikada Daiva Koraga Taniya, Shree Babbuswamy Adhyayana Kendra (Kannada)

Gurupura, R. (2017). Tulunada Mayakarer, Akshari Prakashana (Kannada)

Sturrock, J. (1894). Madras District Manual: South Canara (Vol. 1), Madras Government Press

Unnikrishnan, E. (2023). Uttarakeralathile Vishudhavanangal, DC Books (Malayalam)

Shastri, J.L. (1950). The Shiva Purana,, Motilal Banarsidas

Chaturvedi, R. (2004). Shrinetratantram, D.P.B. Publications (Hindi)

Ghost, M. (1951) The Natyasastra (ascribed to Bharata Muni), The Royal Asiatic Society of Bengal

Wrangham, R (2010) Catching Fire: How Cooking Made Us Human, Basic Books

Articles Referred

Hindu, T. (2016, December 5). 175 glorious years for Basel Mission Press. Retrieved from The Hindu: https://www.thehindu.com/news/cities/Mangalore/175-glorious-years-for-Basel-Mission-Press/article16762961.ece

Deccan Herald. (2022, November 30). Revisiting Paaddana. Retrieved from Deccan Herald: https://www.deccanherald.com/specials/revisiting-paddana-1167140.html

Deccan Herald, N. J. (2015, August 04). Healing Beats of Aati Kalenja. Retrieved from Deccan Herald: https://www.deccanherald.com/content/493155/healing-beats-aati-kalenja.html

Indic Today, V. K. (2021, February 13). Bhoota Aradhane: Where 'Possession' Is An Art. Retrieved from Indica Today: https://www.indica.today/long-reads/bhoota-aradhane-where-possession-art/

BBC Travel, M. J. (2020, November 20). Where bananas are considered sacred. Retrieved from BBC Travel: https://www.bbc.com/travel/article/20201118-where-bananas-are-considered-sacred

Tulu-research blog, Panjurli: https://tulu-research.blogspot.com/2010/03/233-panjurli.html

Widsom Library, Bhuta: https://www.wisdomlib.org/definition/bhuta

IONS Blog, Survival of Consciousness After Death: https://noetic.org/blog/survival-of-consciousness/

Sacred Texts, Mahabharata: https://sacred-texts.com/hin/maha/index.htm

The News Minute. (2022, March 22). Maari to Maariamma. Retrieved from The News Minute: https://www.thenewsminute.com/karnataka/maari-maariamma-brahminising-local-deities-threatens-religious-ties-coastal-karnataka-162649

Tulu Dicitonary: https://tuludictionary.in/dictionary/cgi-bin/web/frame.html

About the Author

K. Hari Kumar is an Indian author and screenwriter who has written seven books including the widely popular *India's Most Haunted* which earned acclaim as a must-read book and secured a spot in HarperCollins India's list of Hundred Best Books by Indian Authors. Hari's narratives, deeply rooted in Indian folklore and regional mythology, have captured the imagination of readers nationwide.

Beyond his literary endeavours, K. Hari Kumar also works as a screenwriter and filmmaker. His novel *The Other Side of Her* was adapted into the acclaimed Hindi language web series *Bhram*.

Educated in Gurugram, K. Hari Kumar holds a B.Tech. in Information Technology and a B.A. in English Literature. Presently residing in Pune with his wife, he remains committed to nurturing his creative pursuits.

Daiva is the first in the series of books by K. Hari Kumar on folk mythology and the occult slated for publication by HarperCollins India.

HarperCollins *Publishers* India

At HarperCollins India, we believe in telling the best stories and finding the widest readership for our books in every format possible. We started publishing in 1992; a great deal has changed since then, but what has remained constant is the passion with which our authors write their books, the love with which readers receive them, and the sheer joy and excitement that we as publishers feel in being a part of the publishing process.

Over the years, we've had the pleasure of publishing some of the finest writing from the subcontinent and around the world, including several award-winning titles and some of the biggest bestsellers in India's publishing history. But nothing has meant more to us than the fact that millions of people have read the books we published, and that somewhere, a book of ours might have made a difference.

As we look to the future, we go back to that one word— a word which has been a driving force for us all these years.

Read.